# Embracing Your Future

*Enhance the Second Half of Your Life with
a Faith-Based Journey of Self-Discovery*

## K A T H Y   H E R R I C K

WESTBOW
PRESS®
A DIVISION OF THOMAS NELSON
& ZONDERVAN

THE HOLY BIBLE, NEW INTERNATIONAL VERSION®, NIV® Copyright © 1973, 1978, 1984, 2011 by Biblica, Inc.® Used by permission. All rights reserved worldwide.

WestBow Press books may be ordered through booksellers or by contacting:

WestBow Press
A Division of Thomas Nelson & Zondervan
1663 Liberty Drive
Bloomington, IN 47403
www.westbowpress.com
1 (866) 928-1240

ISBN: 978-1-9736-0274-3 (sc)
ISBN: 978-1-9736-0273-6 (e)

Library of Congress Control Number: 2017914726

Print information available on the last page.

WestBow Press rev. date: 09/25/2017

# Preface

How do we "do" life? We each grew up watching our parents, teachers, and other significant adults in our lives to gain our clues. Those we watched were mostly in their twenties and thirties, perhaps pushing into their forties, and they were busy raising families, going to jobs, keeping house, spending time with friends, and being involved in outside activities like church, clubs, and sports. If we were lucky to have positive role models, we learned how to be a supportive family member, how to build relationships, and how to be a contributing member of society.

We watched, we learned, we grew up, and we did life. What we probably didn't see clearly was how to do life when life moves into its second half. I think, too, that I didn't want to see it, didn't want to think about my parents in that part of life, didn't want to think about the day when they would be gone, so I didn't. I didn't want to think about my ever being in the second part of my own life, so I didn't.

In our fifties and sixties, changes and transitions happen with rapidity; some we anticipate, but some take us by surprise. Something shook me up, though, as I moved into my fifties: When I tried to use strategies from the past to deal with current ups and downs, they didn't seem to work anymore. Change flipped everything upside down. Who I thought I was suddenly didn't fit any more.

How we defined ourselves for years as we raised families and were a part of the work world changed. How we navigated ups and downs in the past didn't work so well in the present. How we found purpose had shifted or was gone. The changes came firing at us: professionally, personally, emotionally, and physically (I could go on, but I won't). Our self-worth and self-view sometimes took a beating; we were suddenly not in charge, not the leader, not the parent raising children, and not a voice always listened to.

As we move from the first half of life to the second half, we need to deliberately focus on ourselves, past and present, and make decisions about how to live a future with purpose. Most probably, you have many years ahead of you. Improved health care and opportunities have redefined what aging and retirement look like for many people. The goal of this book is to help guide you in that process of self-exploration. It will encourage you to identify what matters to you now and to look at the impact your past experiences have had on you. We will look at the transitions inherent to this time in life and how to move through them in a faith-based manner. We will consider who we are, what God wants us to be, how we build relationships with others, and the importance of relationships and support at this time of life. This is a time of life to fully embrace our faith, to learn more about how God is preparing each of us to be fruitful in the future, and to understand that we have a critical role to play in His mission to the world, right now.

The text of each chapter includes reflection questions and spaces to jot down your thoughts, right in your book. If you are following this study on your own, this format will help guide you to a greater degree of self-understanding and growth. If you are using this book as a part of a group study, you will be ready to share when your group meets. Small groups are recommended, as they are a wonderful place to meet others and get to know them. They also provide an opportunity to support others and find personal support as you each explore your own journey and purpose in the future.

It is important to be there for others. As much as this is about your journey, helping you to better understand yourself, your faith walk, and moving toward your dreams, purpose, service, and legacy, there are times someone else may just need someone to listen, and that someone may be you. There also may be times you need someone to listen to you; the goal is that someone will be there for you too.

So let's go exploring: uncover more about who we are, learn whose we are, and open wide the doors on a faith-filled, purposeful life in this second half of our lives. God has much for us to do. He has joy to surround us with and golden moments to treasure. Embrace the beautiful future God has prepared for you.

Kathy

*Embracing Your Future* is dedicated to the women who have been a part of my life in this, the second half, and who have shown me the love of God through their example, their openness, and their honesty. They have each touched my life and helped me grow, given me insights, and brought to the surface a willingness to open up, listen, find purpose, chase a dream, and take a risk. Herein is the result of these beautiful individuals.

A special thanks to Lynda Ruter for writing and sharing her beautiful prayers which are found at the end of each chapter, and for her inspiration to be open to the possibilities God gives to us.

# Contents

## Chapter 1

# What Matters?

Jesus replied, "Love the Lord your God with all your heart, and with all your soul and with all your mind. This is the first and greatest commandment. And the second is like it, Love your neighbor as yourself."
—Matthew 22:37–39

## What Matters to You?

As I held the fragile vase, a wedding gift to my great-grandparents nearly one hundred and fifty years ago, I gently ran my thumb across the satiny smooth surface. Looking at my hands encircling the vase, I visualized the hands of three other women in our family: my mother, grandmother, and great-grandmother, all passed on now, but each an owner at some point of this vase. I sensed the presence of our four generations, four women, connected by this vase, but more importantly, connected by love, generation to generation.

Like the vase, our lives are fragile. Our time on earth is finite, and time passes quickly. Wasn't it just yesterday we were in our thirties, busy with our jobs, perhaps raising children, leading clubs, and active in other organizations? Blink … and now here we are, retired or soon to be in the near future, many of our roles changed, searching for purpose for the next phase, looking for ways to fill minutes that were previously dedicated to all those responsibilities. Yes, life is fragile and quick, with no guarantee that we will have tomorrow, so it is critical that we carefully examine our lives, determine what it means to live fully, decide what our Lord is asking of us, and focus clearly on what matters today. And then, with laser-like focus, we must match up how we spend our time, talents, and treasures with what matters most to us.

I recently heard a presentation by a woman who survived a fire in her home that took the lives of her parents and her three young daughters. She said that before the fire, she had been concerned about her job and often missed her daughters' activities because of it. She pushed organic foods on them and worried about toys strewn on the floor and unmade beds. Losing her daughters and parents in the fire changed everything; she stopped and pushed aside the rush of daily life. She realized her job, the organic foods, and the neat house didn't matter. It was the love, the conversations, the snuggling, and the moments of just being together that made life worth living. She said she would give anything to have time with her daughters to do it over; their lives would be different, and the way she matched up what she believed mattered and how they all lived their lives would be different. She touched everyone who heard her story.

The goal in this chapter is to uncover what really matters to you. You will be considering ways to structure your life so that your focus, actions, and legacy all match what matters to you.

## Reflection

If your home had a fire, what would you save?

_____

_____

If you knew you had only one day left to live, what would you do? Who would you want to see? What would you want to say?

_____

_____

What might others remember of your life one hundred years from now?

_____

_____

What experiences in your life have changed what you value? In what ways?

_____

_____

## Focus on What Matters; Let Go of What Does Not

When answering "What matters?" the first word for many is "love." God tells us about love: "Love your neighbor as yourself," "For God so loved the world," "Love one another." Love as God loves us, deep in the heart love. With the understanding that love is primary, what else would you answer if asked, "What matters?"

In the second half of your life, you still have a future, a tomorrow, and God still has a purpose for you in your life. It's a time many people stop and look back, rifling through old pictures and mementos, perhaps studying genealogy, reading old journals, remembering, thinking, and feeling. It's a time to look in the rear-view mirror and try to understand who you were in the past and what mattered to you then, a time to examine successes and difficulties, to look carefully at changes and transitions. Those big moments stand out, but take a minute to let yourself remember those everyday times: average days, the natural rhythm that was your daily life. These small moments may not have seemed important: the opportunity to touch a shoulder, to whisper, "I love you," kiss a scraped knee, listen to a dream; days of normalcy matter. Normal is where joy lives; it is where smiles come easily and where God provides opportunities to touch the lives of others. Live in the moment; all the moments matter.

Today is a good time to reflect on your own life and decide what matters at this stage of your life and what does not. Use that information to choose how to live in the future. What matters? Recognize it, verbalize it, and live it.

## Action Item

List what matters to you and what doesn't. Identifying both can guide you in modifying your use of your time, talent, and resources to focus more clearly on what matters to you. Take action. Choose one thing that matters to you and make one change that will show it is a priority for you.

## What Matters: A Walk through Life

> I thought it was living in the big house on the corner,
> I learned it was the love of family in our little house.
>
> I thought it was wearing the best name brand clothes,
> I learned it was having the clothes I needed each season.
>
> I thought it was making the cheerleading team,
> I learned it was having friends to have fun with.
>
> I thought it was having the best grades in class,
> I learned it was having a good educational experience.
>
> I thought it was about a cute boyfriend on my arm,
> I learned it was about a loving, faithful husband.
>
> I thought it was about having a child who was popular,
> I learned it was about having a child who is kind.
>
> I thought it was about a perfectly kept house,
> I learned it was about spending time with family.
>
> I thought it was about having a sporty new car,
> I learned it was about having transportation.
>
> I thought it was about the best job with high pay,
> I learned it was about having enough to care for my family.
>
> I thought it was about being famous and popular,
> I learned it was about having deep, close friendships.
>
> I thought it was about what the world thinks and dictates,
> I learned it was about God's word and His will for us.

I thought it was about all the stuff I have and wanting more,
I learned it was about having enough and being content.

I thought it was about trying to be the best at everything,
I learned it was about serving others selflessly.

I thought it was about controlling everything in my life,
I learned it was about loving God and letting Him be in control.

I thought it was all about me,
I learned it is all about Him.

Faith matters.


## My Prayer

Lord,

Thank You for today, as I begin my journey through understanding the past, living in the present, and preparing for my future purpose. Thank you for the opportunity to pause and reflect, examine, and purposefully look ahead to embrace my future. Help me have an open mind and open heart to meet the challenges and possibilities in this study. I pray that You will guide me continually through this study. Show me how I can change and grow. Teach me how I can live more fully by thinking about what is really important and who I want to be, who You want me to be.

In Jesus's name,

Amen

# Chapter 2

# Looking Back: Learning, Cherishing, Letting Go

Forget the former things, do not dwell on the past. See, I am doing a new thing!

—Isaiah 43:18–19a

## A Time of Significant Change

The second half of life is a time of tremendous change in our lives. We retire; we leave our jobs and the security of knowing where we will be going almost every day. Our children grow up, and the definition of "Mom or Dad" and how we are needed changes drastically, especially after they say, "I do." We may physically move, leaving behind not only a house but memories, friends, and the familiar. Relationships may change or even fall apart. We may face health issues ourselves, or a loved one may be fighting a serious illness. We face the death of a spouse, parent, relative, or good friend. Throw in the changes we see in the mirror and how we feel as we climb out of bed, and I believe this stage of life requires one to deal with more changes of all kinds (physical, mental, emotional, social, environmental, and spiritual) than at any other time of our lives.

How do we move through all of these changes? These are times when we may begin to feel we no longer know how to do life in a way that brings us hope and purpose in the future. We search for something that tells us that life is not over; it is just different, and God has important plans for us. How do we look back, learn from the past, learn from today, and turn to face tomorrow with a positive attitude? How can we doggedly refuse to let what was yesterday define tomorrow? How can we look at tomorrow as a possibility, full of potential and joy?

"Brothers and sister, I do not consider myself yet to have taken hold of it. But one thing I do: Forgetting what is behind and straining toward what is ahead, I press on toward the goal to win the prize for which God has called me heavenward in Christ Jesus" (Philippians 3:13–14).

This chapter will explore our pasts. We carry with us a sum total of those experiences that brought us to today, but we will look at how they have both held us back and prepared us to fly ahead, and how using an understanding of both will help us set our purpose and move ahead in the future.

## Learning the Lessons of Yesterday

Be courageous, be open, be willing to honestly look back, to chat with God, to say, "Okay, I've been through this situation, what would you have me learn? What is there that You would have me remember—not cling to, but remember—so that when You send me to help someone in the future who is also in this situation, I will remember the feelings, the experience, and how I moved successfully through it?"

As you look at those experiences, some are just what was, and now your life is different; it's just a change. You used to drive a sports car, then it was a station wagon, and maybe it's a sports car again (although it might be a challenge to climb in and out of those low-slung things). These changes are not bad or difficult; they are just different. But at other times, when we look back, it's something painful. It may be losing a loved one, facing an illness, losing a job, or more. But consider the pain of clinging to those circumstances, clinging to those feelings of loss and pain, and never letting go of them. Often, there can be greater pain when you grip whatever was back there in your past than the challenge of letting go of it. As hard as it is to accept, what is past is past; it can't be changed. It's over, and it's not coming back. Don't let your eyes be glued to the past; you aren't going there.

When my mom died, it was after years of debilitating illness; during those years, I struggled, watching her struggle with the challenges, while trying to do what I could to help her. When she was first diagnosed with a Parkinsonism disease, I was angry. I wanted my "real" mom, not the one suffering from dementia and physical disabilities. I wanted to run around with her, have coffee together, talk on the phone, just hang out together, but all that was gone. At some point, I think God whispered to me, "No matter what you want, Kathy, she is not going to regain her health again, will never be that mother again." It was a bitter pill to swallow and it took me time to grieve the loss of that relationship. But it helped me understand that others must be allowed time to grieve, for I do believe we grieve when we let go, going through the varied stages of grief, in our own way and on our own timeline. I believe we grieve the loss of the significant ones in our lives, but also the loss of our jobs, loss of our roles, the death of dreams, the loss of expectations.

A few years ago, my son experienced a divorce and his words to me, in the midst of that divorce, were so telling: "I am grieving the death of my dreams, Mom. I believed when I married that we would have a happy life together, that we would raise children in a happy loving environment together, and that is far from what is true now. I need time, I need time to grieve those dreams."

As I watched him let go of that dream and begin to heal, I also saw him reaching for and finding happiness and peace in his life, but it took time. God is patient. He gives us time to heal; He does not abandon us.

## Letting Go

Letting go. So much is hard to let go of: a safety wire, your money, your dreams, the rope in tug-of-war, your children. All seem pretty challenging and full of difficult emotions, and yet, if we never let go of the past, we will never find the wonderful future God has prepared for us.

Letting go is not ignoring your past experiences, pretending those days and times never happened. Letting go is accepting that both the difficult and positive days of your life, are a part of who you are. Letting go is not loosing your past, it is choosing to not let it define your future.

Letting go is removing the grip the past may have on you. Feelings of sadness, regret, frustration, anger or jealousy are left behind. It brings a clearing of emotion, a peace that allows you to push aside the tentacles that would hold you back, allows you to examine and learn from your past, empowers you to move forward.

When you let go, you are freed to embrace your memories in a healthy way, cherishing those that are special, learning from your experiences and not clinging to those that are difficult. You accept that what is past is past. You accept that your past is a part of your human journey, a part of your growth to today, but that it will not take away your future.

Letting go of the past takes courage, strength, and being your own best friend, and in doing so, freeing yourself to embrace a future of possibilities.

Consider too, that letting go also has to do with the small frustrations in our lives that we all run into on a daily basis. A friend may be late, a driver may cut us off, a spouse may forget to lock the door, a workman may be late and more. We have a choice in those moments too, to let those instances get under our skin, wash unwanted feelings over us, or to respond with patience and calmness, and to let those instances go. Life is too short to let every day frustrations take away our choice to be joyful. Let those little frustrations go, don't let them color your moments and days.

## Cherish, Don't Cling

Does letting go mean that you must forget your past? Absolutely not. There are many wonderful memories that we all carry that are a gift from God. We have friends and experiences we should be thankful for and cherish. They are treasures of our past and close to our hearts. They are a distinct part of who we are. People in our past leave imprints on us, and we are right to cherish warm loving memories.

But there are times we hang on so tightly to our past, both warm memories and difficult ones, that we are unable to move into the beautiful future God has for us. We reach out and grab ahold of those memories, winding our fingers around them, clutching them so tightly that no one can pry open our grasp. You may be clinging to people, experiences, places, even grudges, hurt, or anger. Clinging keeps you in one place, keeps you from the joy God has for you, and keeps you from seeing His purpose for you in the future. Cherishing allows you to treasure the past and yet still move forward in your life.

## Fear

One of the great constants of life is change. Just as we become complacent and settle in, something changes, and often, as humans, we want to push away change and stay in the sameness that we are used to. The challenge of something different can be scary and frightening, and when it comes with the loss of a relationship, loved one, job, or way of life, it can even immobilize us.

The fear of the unknown keeps some people from moving forward. The familiar feels like the best because one knows and understands it. What's ahead is in the shadows and may not be clear. If you are facing retirement, what your life is going to look like, what your passions may be, or how you will spend your time, may be unclear. You may hang on tightly to that job, even though you no longer need it or have a passion for it. If you need to move out of the home you have lived in for a very long time, you may fight to stay there because it's what you know and where the memories are. When you are stuck in fear and fighting change, you may refuse to look at other options in your life.

God knows fear can be a destructive emotion, leaving you stuck in place, like standing in the hardened cement, unable to move, but quaking and wavering in that place. "Fear not …" is found more often in the Bible than any other command, and the only way to truly let go of that kind of fear is to turn to God. He alone can bring you peace, settle your worries, help you see clearly the changes you must make, and give you the confidence that you will survive the unknown just fine. God was with you in the past, He is here with you today, and He will be with you in the future: yesterday, today, and tomorrow.

"The Lord himself will go before you and He will be with you, He will not leave you or forget you. Don't be afraid, don't worry" (Deuteronomy 31:8).

## Be Open to the Future

Think about how much of your energy goes into hanging onto something that is already passed. Your mind, physical being, hopes, dreams, and creative energy are all wound up in that or are mired down by it. When you let go and open up to a future that is different, it can bring on a healthier existence in all ways in your life: physically, mentally, socially, spiritually, intellectually. You are free: free to explore, to wonder, to see potential in absolutely everything. You are free to think about your gifts and talents and how you want to use them. You are free to choose to make today the "some day" that you always are referring to. Some day … it's today.

You can be re-energized when you let go; you can be ready to start over, open to new ideas and learnings, open to exploring other options and activities, open to seeing the world and being more aware in all ways. You can open up to God, to the gentle way He whispers to you, to finding Him in others, to walking gently with Him out in His natural world. You may very well believe that you understood life in the past, but when you let go and open up, you may just find the real meaning of life is in the future.

## Reflection

What are you holding on to from your past?

_____

_____

What change or transition has been the most difficult for you to move through?

_____

_____

## Moving Ahead

Moving ahead with confidence is a deliberate process. You need to recognize what is holding you back, what difficulties there have been or what you had in your past that perhaps you loved, but is done, that you need to let go of. You need to have some self-talk, remind yourself that it is finished, and it's time to be healed if it was a problem, to be motivated on if it was not, and that God has a purpose for you in the future, most probably in a new way. Let it go, in order to let God do His work in you and through you. Your life is like a book. If you keep rereading the same chapter, you will never get to the next chapter. God wants you to turn the page, because He has something exciting in that next chapter for you.

If the past has had a grip on you, loosen it; take some time to consider where you are, what you have learned from the past, what your gifts and talents are, and where God may be leading you in the future. You are God's child. He has a purpose for you, every single day. You may not even know the big picture of His plan, but you can have the confidence of knowing that every day, as you wake up, there is indeed a purpose for you, as His child, in that day. Let go, and move ahead.

Recently, our pastor spoke of the "Fist to Open Hand" prayer, about how there are times we hang on to the past. We hang on to emotions, times, people, situations, that are gone; we hold on so tightly that it is like we have our fist wrapped around them. In this posture, our hands are closed; we are not open to receiving the blessings God may have for us, receiving something new that God may have ready for us. He asks us to relax our fingers, uncurl them, turn our hands over, and let our palms be lifted to God, open and ready to receive, open to God's will and guidance, open to possibilities and a future grounded in Him.

## Our Lord Is Here

Our Lord is here, ready to help us, ready to reach out to us, take away what binds us to the past, give us the strength to turn and move ahead into the future. Our Lord is faithful and trustworthy; He will never forsake us, and He will heal, mold, and mature us in Him. Cherish the lessons of the past but see clearly that life is not finished, that He has an amazing road laid out in front of you. He is there, ready to journey on, right beside you.

## Reflection

What is a time that fear of the unknown stopped you from moving forward?

_____

_____

What do you cherish from your past?

_____

_____

What is something from your past that you cling to that you feel you should let go of?

_____

_____

## Naomi: A Biblical Story of Letting Go and Moving Ahead

Naomi, her story chronicled in the Bible, faced hardship after hardship. Her husband moved their family to Moab, where her sons grew up and married. Tragically, her husband and sons died, and life changed drastically for Naomi. She was in a foreign land, with no protector and no way to care for herself or her widowed daughters-in-law.

Naomi moved through the stages of grief: She was hurt, grief-struck, angry at God and at her situation, but she ultimately turned back to God, letting go of her dreams of being a wife, mother, grandmother, letting go of her life in Moab and with Ruth, her daughter-in-law; she returned "home." She let go; she was willing to start life anew, and ultimately Ruth remarried and had a child. Naomi acted as grandmother to a sweet baby boy who was an ancestor of David, in the lineage of Jesus.

## Hope

"Not only so, but we also glory in our sufferings because we know that suffering produces perseverance, perseverance character and character, hope. And hope does not put us to shame, because God's love has been poured out into our hearts through the Holy Spirit, who has been given to us" (Romans 5:3–5).

Is there anything good about troubles? Paul answers yes. Our troubles can cause us to be patient; through patience, we develop character; and if we have character, we find hope, and hope sustains us as we deal with our troubles. If you think of this process Paul lays out, we begin to see that through our troubles and finding that hope, hope in God, we often find courage and direction. Hope grounds us in God, and it is also the beginning of being able to let go.

Suffering can teach us lessons about ourselves, about life, about the love of God and how to reach out to others. If we are honest, identify, and examine our suffering carefully and don't deny it, we may see that through our experiences, we have been prepared to make life better for both ourselves and for others in the future.

We each need to own what we struggle with, to be honest with our own self and with God. Life is not always a perfectly happy process, but that is part of being human. When we accept that, God can begin to heal us and lead us as we move ahead in hope. Turn to God in your suffering, find the hope He offers, hope rooted in His faithfulness. Lean on our Lord as we let go and move ahead.

## Growing through Adversity

"Now may the God of peace, who through the blood of the eternal covenant, brought back from the dead, our Lord Jesus, that great Shepherd of the sheep, equip you with everything good for doing His will, and may He work in us what is pleasing to Him, through Jesus Christ, to whom be glory forever and ever" (Hebrews 13:20–21).

Beautiful butterflies: I love them. One day, I opened an email from a friend and saw beautiful butterflies sprinkled throughout. I started to read the message with each picture. It told the story of a man watching a butterfly struggling to leave a cocoon. The butterfly seemed to give up, so the man cut the cocoon open, wanting to help, not realizing that the struggle to be born, to come out of the cocoon, was Mother Nature's way to push fluid into the wings of the butterfly so that they would be full, strong, and able to fly. The struggle to come out of the cocoon strengthens the butterfly, makes it able to withstand and deal with life challenges. By taking away the struggle of the butterfly, the man left it unable to fly.

It reminded me of when our twins were born. The boys were born several weeks early, and the doctors were determined that if at all possible, they would come naturally, not by Cesarean, for going through the fight of birth would strengthen their lungs, make them more able to breathe on their own, be able to begin life strong because they had won the fight of birth.

Hebrews 13:20–21 asks God to give us everything we need so that we can be what He wants. Sometimes, what we need has very little to do with our wants, but this scripture asks us to think about what He wants. Something to consider: how do we become strong if there are never challenges, how do we find courage if there's nothing to be courageous about, how do we understand love if we don't have the challenge to love the unlovable? How do we understand the challenge of changes and transitions, of letting go, if we never walk through that ourselves? God is giving us what we need, and in addition, He stands beside us, matching us, step by step.

We have all we need; the butterfly had what it needed; even our struggles are a part of making us strong, preparing us to deal with what the future will bring. Our goal is to not let the struggles beat us down, but to turn to God and let Him lift us up, teach us, grow us, despite the circumstances. May you define the circumstances in your life through the lens of His love and not let circumstances define you.

## Reflection

What is a situation from your past where struggling helped you grow stronger?

_____

_____

"I have called you by name and you are mine.
When you pass through the waters, I will be with you;

And when you pass through the rivers, you will not drown.
When you walk through fire, you will not be burned, the flames will not hurt you.
You are precious to me, I give you honor, and I love you.
So don't be afraid, I am with you" (Isaiah 43:1b, 2, 4a, 5a).

## Action Item

Consider what you have learned from the past. Identify one way you could help someone living in that same situation now. Take action. Reach out to them today.

## My Prayer

Lord,

Thank You for a lesson that moves me closer to the plans You have for me. I pray You will help me let go of what hinders me from becoming the woman You want me to be. Please don't let my clinging to the past, fear of change, lack of confidence, or sense of hopelessness impede my progress. Please don't let past wrongs mire me down and disable me in the future. Prepare me to have the courage to accept change. Open me to Your knowledge and wisdom; strengthen and prepare me to move forward and experience the amazing life You have ready for me. Every day, Lord, You have a purpose for me. Help me to let go and let You lead and guide me to that purpose.

In Jesus's name,

Amen

# Chapter 3

# Identities: Who Am I? Whose Am I?

"For I know the plans I have for you," says the Lord, "Plans to prosper you and not harm you, plans to give you hope and a future."
—Jeremiah 29:11

## The Picture that Is You

Open your wallet and take out the cards we all carry around. Lay them out; what do they say about you? If that was all someone saw, who would they say you are? Would they say "seasoned" (i.e., older) because there's an AARP card, or would they think you shop all the time because you have lots of credit cards and store loyalty cards? Would they think you are just the information on your driver's license, your attributes (hair color, eye color, etc.)? Would they decide you are friendly or not (are you smiling in that picture)? Would this be who you are, or are you much more than what is in your wallet?

Identity is often seen as behaviors, personal characteristics, ways a person may be similar to others in a group. Some may see it as their personal attributes: where they grew up, the kind of house they live in, the kind of car they drive. Others may use roles as labels for identity: I'm a policewomen, I'm a mother, I'm a store clerk.

Modern life can seem fragmented, hurried, confusing; not much seems permanent in our lives, but when we define ourselves as a member of a group, we are seeking permanence. In reality, permanence in this life is a myth, for life is ever changing. Those roles, memberships, jobs, all disappear. Those children grow up; our looks, our addresses—however you define what gives you identify—all can change or disappear. The only constant is change and our Lord. Perhaps our questions should not be "Who am I?" but "Whose am I?" and "Why do I matter? What difference do I make?"

## Who Were You?

"I know you, you're Joe's mom!" "I know you, you're my brother's teacher!" I know you, you live next door to my friend." Identities and labels: We all wear them, carry them, others define us by our life roles: a daughter, student, ball player, musician, neighbor, and more. There are defining labels that come from our roles in the family, profession, pastimes, pursuits, church work, and more. Roles and identities … and when those roles end, who will others say we were?

A defining moment for me came in my mid-fifties, just as I retired. No longer did the words teacher, principal, educator fit. My youngest two children had just married, and the label "Mom" had changed drastically. My mom had become very disabled; she didn't know who I was, wasn't always sure she was my mom, and so my role as daughter had eroded and disappeared. Life as I'd known it, who I was, as I had defined myself for decades, was suddenly all upside down and no longer accurate. I was at a loss to know how to move forward, for the definitions that gave me direction and purpose were gone or very different than before.

It took this painful period to help me realize that our true identify, who we are at the core, has little to do with outward defining identities put on us or we put on ourselves. When circumstances change, those identities can evaporate, and we can be left empty and dangling. I had known how to do life, how to be a teacher, run a school building, be a daughter and a mom, but no one wanted, needed, or allowed me to do those things any more. I realized I no longer knew how to do life and felt myself crying out, "Who am I?"

I believe God opened my eyes, heart, and mind to the possibility that all those other roles had nothing to do with who I am at my center. In that moment, the ah-ha came, the still voice: "Kathy, you are My child, period."

I literally looked up, incredulous, and said, "That's all?"

He answered, "What more do you need? Being My child is everything. All else in your life must revolve around that."

For the first time in my life, I got it. All the other roles were just that: roles. My identify, who I truly am, is God's child … period.

As you consider that your previous roles may no longer define you, consider that your true identity is not a role but rather a sense of who you are deep in your soul. I am God's child. What does that mean, exactly? Who are you as God's child? Who are you in Christ? In Christ, we are so many wonderful things.

Following are several ideas that may help you gain a better understanding of your identify in Christ. As you read each idea, consider what it means in your life. Then write your personal reflection about each idea. When you are finished with this chapter, you will have a much deeper understanding of your most important role or identity at this time in your life: your role as God's child. With your identity in God, He takes you to His heart and provides you with powerful support.

## Who Am I in Christ? Cared For

### John 6:35–38

Our bedroom door doesn't close tightly and there's a sliver of light, along the edge of the door, from a nightlight in the hall. I look at that sliver and think about my comfort in knowing the light is there; darkness can't overtake me. I just have to open the door to have more light, but it's up to me to do that. It's the same with our Lord. He is always there, His light is ever present, constant. We just need to open our door, our heart, and let His light shine in. He is ever willing to care for each one of us.

## Reflection

How has God has cared for you? What blessings have you seen in your life, even in times of trouble? How can you pass it on, care for others too?

_____

_____

_____

## Who Am I in Christ? A Wonderful Creation

**Genesis 2:7**

I rummaged in the basement, looking for crafts for my granddaughter to do: tin can pencil holders; paper flower bouquets; paper, scissor, and glue possibilities, creating. My sister creates artistic items, my dad painted, my mom decorated houses to rival HGTV, and me? Well, someone has to be the appreciator. Retirement has given me time to look around and see how creative others are: quilting, making jewelry, painting, woodworking, singing, and more.

The greatest creator is God. He takes dust, no fancy materials or tools, gently breathes into us, and here we are: all parts working (most of the time) and beautiful in form. Our personalities, traits, and gifts are varied. He has created talents in each of us: music, art, hospitality, working hands on, solving problems, comforting, and more. We are a complexity of moving parts, with a soul, mind, and heart. He has created each of us as unique beings, with a unique mission for His Kingdom.

Celebrate! You are His wondrous creation, made so He can love, treasure, and bless you, made to share friendship with Him, and for you to work beside Him to make the world a better place. You are His blessed creation; be the appreciator.

## Reflection

What are the unique traits, gifts, and talents that God has created in you? How can you use them in His mission for you in this world?

_____

_____

## Who Am I in Christ? His Child

**Psalm 139**

I watch faces; people intrigue me and I try to think about how they live, what matters to them, how life for them might be different (not wrong, just different). Psalm 139 is powerful; no doubt, we are each His child. He is there for each of us, in the good and bad times, highs, lows, healthy, sick, sad, or joyful; always He is there. Our Lord wants to claim every single person on this earth.

Being God's child is different than being the child of our earthly parents; they come close, with their love, care, and concern, but our Lord is so in tune with us, His greatest creation, that He knows our innermost thoughts, feelings, wants, and needs. We can't hide; God knows all of it. In the same way, we can silently talk to Jesus. He hears, knows, and understands. We can have lots of little one-on-one conversations about anything, and I think that's the kind of conversation He likes best.

His child: secure, loved, known inside and out, given grace, forgiven.

## Reflection

When can you make time for quiet talks with God? How can you respond to others differently, knowing we are all children of God?

_____

_____

## Who Am I in Christ? New

### Philippians 3:20–21

Mirrors. Lately, my mirror has been sharing with me that the passage of time is becoming more clearly etched on my face. With these changes, it's challenging to not be caught up in seeing youthful physical appearance as our only definition of beauty and obsessing about trying to look younger. If we spend all our time worrying about this, we lose the essence of what God is telling us here.

If we are His, this body will pass away, and we will have a new body; the trappings of life on this earth will fall away. We will be made new; our earthly house may be destroyed, but not without God having that heavenly one ready for us. Jesus became flesh, lived as a man, in a human body with feelings, joys, challenges, hurts, injuries, illness. He then put aside the earthly body and is now with God in heavenly form. He holds this out for us too, if we have faith and trust.

As I watched my dad's last five months and my mom's last few years; it hurt so much to see their earthly bodies causing them pain and suffering. I also know how beautiful it is to be certain that they are now with God in heaven, having put aside their "earth suits" and slipped on gossamer wings and beautiful, heavenly bodies. We can have confidence that a new suit awaits each of us in heaven.

## Reflection

How can you put aside worry about your earthly body and concentrate instead on your heavenly body awaiting you in the future?

_____

_____

## Who Am I in Christ? I Am in the Family

**Romans 8:15–16**

The family: Genealogy intrigues me. I love history, relationships, and seeing how the two intertwine together. We learn something about ourselves through learning about our ancestors. The family of the past: Some were powerful, some virtually unknown, some scrabbled in the dirt, some dressed in kilts, some were lucky to have a pair of pants to wear. But they're family, all interconnected, the DNA, the traits, spiraling down through generations, until the mixture that's us arrives on earth.

But family is not defined just by DNA, rather by love, care, concern, and being there. It is that day-in-and-day-out presence, the willingness to drop the "I wants" when others in the family have "I needs." It's a willingness to make hard decisions and choices when you know it is best for the other person. It is putting aside self and focusing instead on others. Family will have your back, no matter what.

God welcomes us into His family, and all the most positive aspects of family are available from our heavenly Father and fellow Christian family members. These family members come alongside during the hard times, reaching out to share love, care, and concern. They are willing to listen, even when they have heard our troubles before; they will help us celebrate good times, cry with us when it hurts, share, talk, listen, make the casseroles, mow the lawns, or whatever it takes to be there, to have each other's back, to be family. God's child. God's family; what a family.

## Reflection

How do you feel, knowing that you are a child of God? What can you do to share love with others, as a member of God's family?

_____

_____

## Who Am I in Christ? A Possibility

**Matthew 19:26**

The figure jumped out of the box. I jumped, every single time, even though I knew what would happen and the place in the song where it would happen. I was still startled and still jumped, and I didn't like it. I like to know what's going to happen and usually help orchestrate it. I like to be prepared, over-planned, and to be honest, I have been giving God hints throughout my life, about how things should go.

But God isn't going to stay in the box, no matter where in the song we are, and isn't afraid to startle us. That's good. If our lives are so well ordered, so planned out in human terms, we will miss the amazing possibilities He has for us.

We are vibrant, pulsating possibilities for God; amazing things can happen through us, in our homes, neighborhoods, churches, communities, world. A friend told of spontaneously comforting someone, having felt God's nudge. She was living out her possibility. Others do mission work, trusting God for support; others volunteer even when they don't have time to and find God has great things for them to do. The possibilities can be words, notes, emails, time, sharing talents, having patience, building relationships, big responsibilities, or little ones. They can be small moments and big events. They can be a kindness in the store or committing oneself to stand by a friend until the end. Everything God puts in our paths has the potential for us to use the possibilities He has planted in us. We need to get the lid off the box, be open and ready all the time, be listening, be willing to act. Let go and let God.

## Reflection

Where do you see God opening up possibilities in your life? How can you encourage others to let God's possibilities for them unfold?

_____

_____

## Who Am I in Christ? Sealed with the Holy Spirit

### Ephesians 1:13

Jesus died on the cross; the earth moved. His followers' souls, racked with pain, saw it unfold but could not believe He was anything other than dead and sealed in the tomb. They felt their hope was sealed inside that tomb too; they felt they had been abandoned, but God knew better.

The stone was rolled away; Jesus emerged, and after several appearances, He ascended into heaven. But, it's not us here and Jesus there; we are not abandoned. We are not alone. He has left the Holy Spirit with us and sealed us with His love through the Holy Spirit. It is this steadfast love that is with us until we are redeemed, until He calls us home to Him.

People talk about the Holy Spirit being in us, and I try to picture that, but the image I have is being surrounded by the Holy Spirit: kind of in a bubble, being nurtured, cared for, kept safe, having wounds from the world's arrows bounce off, reflected by the Spirit's protecting presence. God's gift: the Holy Spirit.

## Reflection

How can you be more confident in your life because the Holy Spirit is ever with you?

_____

_____

## Who Am I in Christ? Secure

### Romans 8:28–39

The word security brings to mind Linus, in the comic strip *Peanuts*, dragging his security blanket around. Scripture tells us that the saving grace of Jesus as our security blanket, wrapped lovingly around us, is all we need.

If we are His, we can't be separated from Him. If you look at what matters, if God is for us, does it really matter who is against us? We can know the depth of His love for us, how great His commitment is to us, because He allowed His Son, Jesus, to die for us. No matter what arrows and slings come from others, from situations, from health care issues, from day-to-day challenges, God is in our corner. We may go through tough times, but with God in and with us, around us like that blanket, we won't be destroyed.

There's nothing on earth—no person, situation, joy, sorrow, war and more—that can separate our hearts from God. Live life surrounded by His security.

## Reflection

What do you need to lay at God's feet, that you find challenging?

_____

_____

## Who Am I in Christ? Blessed

### Matthew 5:3–11

I wandered about the house, put in a load of laundry, made coffee, put things away, checked the to-do list; slowly, it began to permeate my mind that these blessings we keep talking about God bestowing on us are often mundane, everyday things, while in our human way, we keep looking for big, grandiose things, like a new car or house, a windfall of money, an amazing job, or a miracle cure.

God let me get up out of my bed today under my own power. He gave me clothes to wear, a washer to wash them in, and electricity that I trusted to come on. The coffee is percolating; the computer is humming. I stopped to look at the peace lily my cousin sent me when my mom died, reminding me of my mother's and my cousin's love. I began to see that blessings come in all shapes and sizes: in the ordinary moments, moments of quiet and just being, through the people He has placed in our lives.

These are blessings in human terms, but the greatest blessings of all are spiritual. He blesses us daily in a multitude of ways, but the spiritual blessings He offers us, the blessing of having a God who cares about each of us, loves us, and promises us life everlasting, are the greatest ones of all. Consider just how very blessed we all are, as His. Thanking God.

## Reflection

What blessings can you point out in your life right now? What blessings can you see as you look back at your life? How will you act on the knowledge of His spiritual blessings in your life?

---

---

## Who Am I in Christ? God's Helper

### Genesis 2:19–24

Sometimes, being God's helper means being right there with someone, side by side, lifting when the other can't lift, carrying loads when you know the other has reached their limit. There are also times when we need to enable others, by stepping back. This doesn't mean we ignore them or turn our backs, but rather that we stand close, listen, ask questions, give some insight, but ultimately give that person wings, let them take the step, pick up the load, realize just how much they can do with Jesus.

Helping: So many definitions, but sometimes, it is not easy to know what kind of help to give. Pray, listen, observe, try to look beyond today, pray more, and be there. Whatever you do in God's name, in love, care, and compassion, will be fine. Sometimes, there seems to be no good option, but trust and make the best decision you can.

Helping: being God's hands, feet, voice, and heart on earth. This is our mission.

## Reflection

What is one way you can help others by lifting their load and taking it on as yours? What is a way you can help others by encouraging them?

_____

_____

## Who Am I in Christ? Forgiven

**Romans 3:21–26**

Sheep: The hills and fields of Ireland and Scotland are dotted with them—mammas, babies, fat ones, thin ones, varied colors, some with fluffy coats, some shorn. Every menu had lamb or mutton on it, and woolen stores were everywhere. When we visited, we watched a dog work the sheep, saw a farmer shear sheep, and heard the bleats of sheep from the shores of Ireland to the highlands of Scotland.

The analogy of sheep is often used in the Bible. People in Jesus's time understood the relationship between a shepherd and his sheep, understood the need to be like sheep, with Jesus as the shepherd. If we go astray (sin), He'll herd us back. If we are out of the pasture, charging out of the gate, eating of the apple, if we get tangled in the barbs, it is our Jesus who comes to find us, pulls us out of troubles, brings us back, and forgives us. Back with the herd/family, we aren't perceived as any different than the other sheep who stayed. He forgives us and washes away our sins.

Only our Jesus can totally forget our sin, view us as new. He loves us and encourages us to live the life He has for us; grace, just ask. He will forgive you.

## Reflection

When is a time you found yourself out in the brambles? Is there anything you need to ask God to forgive you for?

_____

_____

## Who Am I in Christ? Living a New Life

**Romans 6:4**

I'm picturing our oldest son, hurrying down a hospital corridor, carrying his firstborn, love shining on his face as he carefully cradled her in his arms. A new life, full of possibilities, full of potential, a babe in arms, ready to be loved and cared for, taught, and molded. When we accept Christ, there is a similar image that comes to my mind: our Lord carrying us, with His face wreathed in love for us. We have found a new life, full of possibilities and potential; we are ready to be loved, cared for, taught, and molded.

We do have a past; that is not negated, but He asks us to bury our sins through His grace, to cherish and not cling to the past, and to be willing to trust Him and look to today, with a new purpose and a new core in our very being. What will we base our actions and our words on? What will be at our very core and motivate us, in our new life, as His? It is our Lord.

The new life is a great one; when you give, it comes back tenfold. When you love, love surrounds you too. When you put others first, you are also filled to the brim. When you use Jesus as your yardstick, there is joy and peace and love. Will life be perfect in this new life? Will it always be easy? Absolutely not. But He will keep making you new through grace and forgiveness, which He asks us to display to others as well. He will be there to carry us through the valleys and celebrate with us in good times. A new life, starting over, brand new, potential, possibilities … and today is a new day.

## Reflection

What do you see as your potential and possibilities in this day? How can you live so that others understand that you have found new life in Him?

_____

_____

## Who Am I in Christ? One Who Follows His Will

### Romans 13:8–10

Think of those goofy glasses we put on as kids. Some rims were wild colors or shapes like stars; some had eyeball lens that popped out. Some were funky lenses with crazy ways to look at the world. But as we look at the world each day, just what should our lens be, as Christians? Love.

Love: That's it. When we think about what to say, say it in love. When we decide how to act, use love as the yardstick. His will for us is love; His love for us, ours for Him, and ours for our neighbors (who indeed should be everyone; if we ride this planet together, at the same time, we are neighbors).

Love: Consider what would Jesus do; lean on the one who loves you more than anyone else in the world, and love Him back. Love your neighbor.

## Reflection

What do you see as His will for you now and in the near future?

_____

_____


## Who Am I in Christ? Glorifying God

### Ephesians 1:12–14

I loved summer camp. I loved spending the week with my buddies from our little church, swimming, doing crafts, singing, being around the campfire, sleeping in cabins; we even put up with those dreaded spiders. I remember when I was about fourteen, asking my camp counselor why God bothered to create man; why would He want us? Her answer was one of three words, "To glorify Him." I've never forgotten that. We ask, plead, tell, get angry at, try to control, shake a fist at, wonder about God, but what about the praising, the glorifying, the realization that He is our all-seeing, all-possible God who loves us to distraction. He is amazing.

Praise Him in song, prayer, sharing, reading His word, reading messages about Him, appreciating His blessings, in all that you have, are, and do. "Praise God from whom all blessings flow; Praise Him all ye creatures here below; Praise Him above ye heavily host; Praise Father, Son and Holy Ghost! Amen." Next time you sing this, truly think about the words, and praise Him.


## Reflection

What is a way you can praise God today?

_____

_____


## Who Am I in Christ? Complete

### Colossians 2:9–10

There was a hole in the middle. Dad and I had stayed up until the wee hours, trying to finish the jigsaw puzzle, using all the pieces, but there was still a hole in the middle. We checked the box and looked around the edges; I crawled around on the floor, but no piece. It was incomplete, not the whole picture, and we both felt a bit deflated; all that work, and it was not complete. That's us without Jesus: a nice-looking picture, nice people, trying to do nice things, but if that important center piece, our Jesus piece, is missing, we are not complete.

Jesus stands right there, holding out the piece; there's no shaking out the clothes looking for it, scrabbling around on the floor, accusing your sister of taking it. It's right there in His hand, waiting for you to reach out and take it. Put Him in the center of your life; complete the picture of you. Then let Him bring you full circle, complete His promise in you—not just today, but forever.

## Reflection

What pieces in your life can Jesus help you fit in better, with Him at the center of your life?

_____

_____

## Who Am I in Christ? Alive

### Colossians 2:13

My dad, a gardener, worked to instill in us an appreciation of what the earth gives us. He felt dirt on our hands was good, a badge of tending to God's world. He helped us see the miracle of going from the blank canvas of dirt in the spring to ripe, plump vegetables and the showy ladies in the rows of flowers of August.

It started with tiny seeds: little potentials of life he let us hold in our hands, moving beside him, dropping them into the holes he prepared. We covered them with dirt, burying each from sight, trusting Dad that something good was going to come from each one, if we tended them. The sun and soil did their work; we watered if the rains didn't come, and I remember our squeals of delight when tender green shoots would start reaching up through the surface of the garden. Alive: Those dormant little dead seeds had really been alive; they just needed the right ground to lie in and the right tending.

That's us: dormant little seeds, sometimes looking like we've given up on life, drab, dried. But if we give ourselves to the Maker; let Him plant us in love; trust His tending; let Him surround us with His grace, kindness, compassion, and blessings, we will grow, sprout, be the tender young plant pushing forth, the mature plant bearing fruit. If we soak up His light and warmth, let ourselves be nurtured in His word, listen to and watch for Him, if we are fed and watered through worship and Bible reading, prayer, and sharing with others, we can truly be alive, eager to share our fruit, the beauty of our flowers, our lives, with others. We are alive in Jesus. Live like it is August.

## Reflection

What fruit has God grown in you so that you can share with others? What beauty can you share with someone who is having a difficult time in life?

_____

_____

## Who Am I in Christ? A Heavenly Citizen

### Ephesians 2:19–22

My speech gave me away, and my tennis shoes, t-shirts, and jeans: I was an American. As an exchange student in Europe, one of the most frequent statements to me was, "You're an American." There was no doubt I was a citizen of the United States, told by my accent, language, clothes, mannerisms, the way I perceived the world.

We are citizens in God's Kingdom, here on earth as the Holy Spirit works through us and in our future forever home in heaven. Can others tell we are God's children by how we live, what we say, how we treat others, what priorities we have? Can they tell what our citizenship papers are, what color our passport is, where we will be going home to after our lifetime journeys on this earth? Are we identifiable as His citizens?

## Reflection

How will others recognize you as a citizen of God's Kingdom?

_____

_____

## Who Am I in Christ? One Who Inherits

### Ephesians 1:9–11

My own will spells out where my money and stuff is supposed to go: a piece of paper to be used when I am gone, no longer with any control. But we find God's will detailed in the Bible. We find His guidance for today and His will for our lives after that last breath. We find that our greatest inheritance is at that moment, when we are taken home to heaven to be with Him forever.

His will for us on earth: offer this inheritance to others. His will for us in the future: that we move through the shadows, cross the river, see our beloveds who have gone ahead, see Jesus's outstretched arms, and know we are home, forever.

## Reflection

What have you done to put your earthly home in order and prepare to inherit Christ's Kingdom?

_____

_____

## Action Item

List roles you play in your life, such as neighbor, volunteer, church member, mother. How will these roles be different with Jesus at the center of your life? Take action. Choose one role and change in how you interact with others.

## My Prayer

Lord,

Thank You for all I have learned so far. I know permanence is a myth; only You are constant. When I remove the roles I had before, I ask, "What is left? Nothing." I have You, and I'm Your child. I need no more; that is everything. Help my life revolve around You; guide me to be patient while You are creating in me a new person, as I grow in Your love. I know I will be an amazing woman with gifts beyond measure in You. Thank You!

In Jesus's name,

Amen

# Chapter 4

# Fruit of the Spirit: God's GPS

But the fruit of the Spirit is love, joy, peace, patience, kindness, goodness, faithfulness, gentleness, self control.
—Galatians 5:22–23a

## Attributes

Attributes: What will people see in us that will tell them we are Christians? When Christ claims us as His, what expectations does He have for us? What behaviors or attributes did Jesus model for us in His earthly time? The song, "They Will Know We Are Christians by Our Love" tells of others watching and seeing behaviors that tell them we are a Christian. As Christians, being aware of these attributes, working to weave them into who we are, living them out on a daily basis in our relationships with others, is a natural offshoot of our faith in Jesus. This chapter will give you more information about each fruit, biblical references, and ideas for weaving them into life.

I started thinking about how many songs there are about the fruit of the Spirit; each subtitle is my effort to weave that in. Having a song in your heart lifts you up; maybe you can think of more examples, perhaps they will be reminders of God's roadmap for us.

## They Will Know We Are Christians By Our Love

### 1 John 4:16, Matthew 22:37–39

The paper hearts were glued on the side of the big white box, pink and red hearts, cut with our little scissors to decorate our class Valentine box. I had entered into the activity eagerly, for into the box would go all our Valentines, and I was hopeful there would be a special one from a little boy named Ronnie, and it would have the word "Love" in his handwriting, on the back. I wasn't disappointed, but at the age of eight, what did I really know of love?

Actually, I think I knew a lot about love, although I wasn't very aware of it. I was very much loved by my family and the church members of our little church, and my teachers and friends were loving and kind. I was a very lucky and blessed little girl at the age of eight. Having Ronnie sign his Valentine with "love" was frosting on the cake.

As I grew up, I began to learn more about love, recognizing there are different kinds of love, and that the most important lesson to learn is that God loves us, that His love is the model for what He is asking of each of us: to love Him back and to love each other.

1 Corinthians 13, often used at weddings, is about selfless love, unconditional love. It is patient, kind, not pompous, not inflated or rude. It doesn't worry about self, is not angry, does not seek revenge or keep a score. It rejoices with the truth, bears all things, believes all things, hopes all things, endures all things. This kind of love never fails.

Agape love, love that is there in abundance and forever, wants nothing but the best for the other person, wanting to help the other person soar, find joy, and be all they can be. Agape love wants nothing in return and is the unconditional love God has for each of us and that He asks us to share with others around us. 1 John 4:16 tells us God is love. Love is the beginning, and all else comes from God's love and our love of God, with all the fruit of the Spirit springing from that love. Consider love the fruit bowl, with all the other fruit in the circle of love.

Think about your life in the past and in the present; consider where you have found and given this kind of love. Was it with your parents, your siblings, a spouse, significant other, children, grandchildren, or someone special in your life? Consider what your feelings were of loving someone so unconditionally. How has that changed your attitudes and behaviors? Have there been times you have reached out to others, in Christ's name, on your mission from Him, with love? Does your love of God transcend everything, is it unconditional, is it free of "Let's make a deal" or "I can be in charge of this" or "Let me tell you how this should go"? If you have not felt this kind of love before, consider how you can find it.

As the song says, "All you need is love."

## Reflection

Who in your life do you love with no thought of yourself or of receiving anything in return?

_____

_____

What can you do, in an observable way, to show love to someone else?

_____

_____

### Ideas for Demonstrating Love

- ☐ Get to know your neighbors and offer to help them.
- ☐ Smile and hug.
- ☐ Make someone feel important.
- ☐ Show concern and kindness.
- ☐ Exhibit hospitality.
- ☐ Keep in touch.
- ☐ Listen.
- ☐ Lift self and others in prayer to the Lord.
- ☐ Be trustworthy.
- ☐ Make positive, loving, and kind remarks to others.
- ☐ Truly care about others and respond to their needs.

## Joy Joy, Joy, Joy, Down in My Heart

### Nehemiah 8:10, Philippians 4:4

Joy from God is deep, heart-felt, and exists no matter what else is happening in your life. It is stable and calm. Even in the midst of losses, sadness, and other difficulties, the joyful person knows God is there, loving and caring. Unlike happiness, it is not transient, not something that comes and goes. True joy comes only from God, our only source of real strength.

Circumstances, what happens, can be good or not, or circumstances can just be the normal routine of the every day. Circumstances can make us happy, like when I find that parking place right next to the store or when the pants I thought didn't fit any more, do. Circumstances can make us unhappy. If I have to pay more taxes, I'm unhappy. If my son says they can't come for dinner, I'm unhappy. The circumstances of my life bring me happiness or take it away. If this circumstantial happiness were the basis of our joy in life, we would be on a perpetual roller coaster of emotions, waiting for each little thing to happen to figure out if we are happy or not.

As Christians, we too face the happiness or unhappiness of circumstances, but we have joy that is independent. We can rise above the circumstances and find ourselves in God's perpetual love all of the time. The Holy Spirit is ever there, no matter the situation: good, bad, normal. Our goal is to keep our focus on God and His love, stretching always toward the purpose He has for us. He surrounds life's circumstances with His love, strength, and joy, offering the gift of Jesus's salvation and grace.

## Reflection

Are your attitudes dependent on the circumstances in your life?

_____

_____

In what circumstance in your life do you need to choose God's joy?

_____

_____

### Ideas for Demonstrating Joy

- ☐ Become joyful as a child.
- ☐ Let go of preconceived ideas.
- ☐ Show acceptance.
- ☐ Celebrate mini successes.
- ☐ Show joy from inside.
- ☐ Have complete immersion into worship at church.
- ☐ Have a lightness of spirit for being alive.
- ☐ Focus on Jesus.
- ☐ Be thankful in all circumstances.
- ☐ Look for blessings in all circumstances.
- ☐ Smile and show joy.

## I Have Peace Like a River in My Heart

**Romans 15:13, Philippians 4:6–7, John 14:27**

We wore matching yellow dresses trimmed in navy blue. Yellow was decidedly not my color, but I was, nonetheless, thrilled to be a member of the chosen-by-audition Youth for Christ Choir, serving mid-Michigan. One of our favorite pieces to sing was "Peace Like a River." Singing it reminded me of sitting by a river, watching the gentle flow of the water, always moving, never static, but so lazy that a leaf could float on the surface for miles. It always calmed me, always seemed to drain the anxieties and stresses, left me feeling like I was just swinging in a hammock, looking up at the sky, watching clouds, just being peaceful.

Thinking of peace in the context of life overall and of the peace that God gives us, the peace that surpasses all understanding, I began to realize that this kind of peace was to be found even in the midst of turmoil. Even when life feels upended, the directions and outcomes unclear, this is the peace that God offers. At the hardest times, we can sink into His peace, and even when we encounter dings and nicks, minor frustrations, we can take a moment, breathe in His peace, let it go, and continue on. His peace completes us, takes away the ragged edges, brings us contentment. We know in His peace that He is in control and that He will care for us.

I love the image of resting in our Lord, of His arms being around us, of being nestled in His lap, of His having a wing over us, sheltering us. We are to fear nothing in the tranquil spot in that moment of peace. We are balanced in His arms and in our lives, if we abide in that peace. It is this kind of peace we see in Christians that allows them to move through difficult situations that might otherwise break them.

Be a peacemaker; be someone who has found peace in the Lord, who understands the gift of completeness that it offers, and then stretch out and offer that to others. In loving God, a natural offshoot is that we love others and offer them support and peace. We are God's hands, feet, voice, and heart, His ministers to the world. God tells us, "Blessed are the peacemakers, for they will be called sons of God." If we have received peace from God, we are to offer peace. We are not to encourage conflict or revenge, anger or resentment, but rather gentleness, kindness, calmness, peace.

## Reflection

Have you found the peace that surpasses all understanding? If not, how can you access that kind of peace?

_____

_____

What is a life situation where you need God's peace?

_____

_____

### Ideas for Demonstrating Peace

- ☐ Show a lack of fear and anxiety.
- ☐ Show calmness.
- ☐ Turn your worry into meditation.
- ☐ Show patience.
- ☐ Communicate with others.
- ☐ Share expectations.
- ☐ Breath slowly and deeply.
- ☐ Touch, lay your hand on someone's shoulder.
- ☐ Listen.
- ☐ Have a Bible verse to repeat as you sit or as you walk.

## Day by Day: Patience

### Ephesians 4:2

It was the toilet seat that set me off; it was up—again. I kind of saw red; my eyes squinted, my tummy clenched, my fists balled up, and the words were coming out of my mouth even before I took a breath: "How many times have I asked you to put the toilet seat down? Why can't you just do that?" He just looked at me, and I stopped, took a breath, and then remembered: I am supposed to be working on patience. For you see, patience is so not my strong suit. Of all of the fruits of the Spirit, this is the one that I really arrived lacking; this is the one that God convicted me to get busy working on, especially at home, especially with Tom.

We live in a rapid-fire society; everything happens quickly. Problems are solved on TV in a half-hour, we are told we are busy people, we are encouraged to do more and more, we don't want to wait for anything. What is the quickest way to get someplace? What is the quickest way to accomplish something? Instant, instant, instant. So while patience can be a challenge, we have to be even more aware, working even harder, because in our society of today, it's a fruit that is challenging to almost everyone. And put a bunch of us together, and you can get the picture that the pot is boiling over even more quickly.

Patience; take a moment to breathe in and think; finding that little moment to decide how you will act or speak can make a huge difference in your relationships and how you get along in the world. Shooting from the hip, saying you speak honestly, is more likely saying you are letting your emotions dictate your responses and not your clear-headed thinking, your reliance on God.

In Exodus 34:6, we read that God is "slow to anger and is rich in kindness and fidelity." Again, we find a model for us as we deal with impatience: slow to anger. God is asking us to bear these wrongs patiently, put up with things that upset us with long suffering. The toilet seat: Well, now, that is not even worth getting upset about, but there are other things in our lives that hurt and upset us. We can choose to react with anger, seething, speaking angry words, seeking revenge, and perhaps driving a wedge between us and the other person forever, perhaps driving that person away from Christ forever, or we can just stop, be quiet, and wait on the Lord.

Several years ago, I was enmeshed in a difficult situation with someone who accused me of blatant untruths. She spoke to me in anger and disrespect; I was shell-shocked. Next came a letter, with most of it untrue, and my first response was anger, then hurt, then a driving urge to write back, to stand up and say how much the accusations and lies hurt. But thank goodness, I sought out a Christian counselor to help me deal with this; her recommendation: do nothing. Pray, be quiet, be calm, focus on the blessings and on what is right in my life, go on with the rest of my life, but don't write back, don't call, don't do anything. How right she was in the recommendation, for my saying nothing, in reality, spoke volumes. In patience, I waited and lived; the situation changed, in God's time and way.

We have all known people who are quick to react, who make snap decisions, whose emotions are near the surface. These people are often called "difficult," and we've all been in situations where their lack of patience has made things difficult for everyone. Consider your own responses when something doesn't go your way. How does that make you feel, physically, emotionally? How does that impact the people around you? Does it make the work of the group, the relationships, move forward, or is your impatience a hindrance? How do we react to impatient people around us? How can we remind them that patience is a virtue, is a fruit of the Spirit, that God is asking us to take a deep breath, let some things go as not being important, and in other situations trust Him and wait for His will and way? I need to let the frustration over the toilet seat go … patience.

## Reflection

Are you impatient? Are you easily irritated? What would your friends and family say? What can you do to work on this?

_____

_____

When your patience is tested, how do you want to respond?

_____

_____

### Ideas for Demonstrating Patience

- ☐ Take calming breaths.
- ☐ Don't be anxious in traffic; be calm, no road rage.
- ☐ Don't worry about getting little things done on time.

&#9633; Be willing to wait for God's answers to prayers.
&#9633; Wait calmly for recovery from illness or injury.
&#9633; Don't speak in anger and frustration.
&#9633; Accept changes in lifestyle as you age.
&#9633; Set long-term goals, see short-term steps.
&#9633; Stay focused on what matters in your life and what doesn't.

## It's Your Kindness

**Ephesians 4:32**

"Be kind to everyone, for everyone has a challenge in their life, even if you can't see it." "When you choose between being right and being kind, choose being kind, for then you will be right." These two sayings are floating around a lot lately; both paint a picture that is true to what God is asking of each one of us as His child, true to the model that He gives us in His treatment of us.

Being kind is to look for ways to make life sweeter for someone else, to make their journey easier, to make their day, to lift their load just a bit. It is focusing on others, not on self, and letting the joy God has gifted you with flow out of you to others. Kindness is not just a feeling; it's action. It is being sweet, gentle, good-natured, friendly, helpful, considerate, and compassionate. Kindness is focusing on the other person with no thought for what is in it for self, with no expectation of being paid back.

My Michigan neighbor is one of the kindest people I know. I see her head out with bouquets of flowers for those suffering difficulties, going to spend time with them. She takes an elderly lady to all her doctor's appointments, drives another to various activities, and was the first one another lady called when her husband died, knowing that my neighbor would be right over to give her emotional support. This neighbor listens to my challenges and hears my concerns and celebrates my joys. She is a kind and compassionate woman; she is not just sweet in her words, she lives that kindness through her actions.

Kindness matters; our kind act in a person's day may seem small or inconsequential to us, but it may be what gets them through that day. Look around; how can we, as Christians, make their day? Is it offering to listen to someone, sit with them, go someplace with them? Is it helping with tasks at home or taking them to the doctor? Is it saying a kind word to a clerk, noticing when someone is doing a good job, commenting on someone's pleasant demeanor? Is it saying a sincere thank you, recognizing what someone has done for us, and letting them know we appreciate it? We can start the ball rolling by being kind.

## Reflection

What act of kindness can you share today with someone else?

_____

_____

**Ideas for Demonstrating Kindness**

- ☐ Share with someone.
- ☐ Check on friends and neighbors.
- ☐ Sit with someone who is lonely; call them and offer to get together.
- ☐ Sincerely care.
- ☐ Be respectful.
- ☐ Smile, wave, acknowledge others.
- ☐ Verbally recognize when someone gives you good service.
- ☐ Take others cookies, send cards and email, help with tasks, make phone calls.

## Surely the Goodness of the Lord Is in This Place

### Ephesians 5:8–9, Psalm 23:6

"Now be a good girl," my mom would admonish me as she left me with a babysitter or dropped me off at Sunday school. I was reading a letter recently from my mom to my gramma. In it, Mom said my older sister used to tease me when I was little, telling me I was not a good girl (she was six; I was two). I guess I would become incensed, stomp my little foot, and declare, "I am too a good girl." Even back then, I knew being a good person was important.

"She's a good person." How often have we heard that description about someone? The first thought that comes to mind is that this person must be kind, but as we examine the essence of goodness, it is more than that. While kindness is to be found within goodness, it is the soft underside to the harder strength of goodness. Goodness is character, integrity, doing what is right; it is a set of beliefs, being willing to live them and act on them in support of others, especially the vulnerable. Jesus shines as our ultimate example of goodness. Goodness comes from a place of strength, not a place of pain and hurt. Goodness is living your life in a way that helps spread God's love, helps stand up for everyone. That's being good.

As we wrap our minds around goodness being something more than kindness, take a mental walk through your life and consider where you have seen goodness being lived out. Where have you seen someone not just talk about caring for others and saying a kind word here and there, but take the additional step of putting aside self to truly minister to that person? Where have you seen someone lift up the vulnerable and stick with it, even in the face of rejection, denial, or obstacles? Where have you seen someone dedicate their purpose to showing God's love and living out that purpose on a daily basis? Where have you found truly good people in your life? In what circumstances have you been called good?

## Reflection

Who was someone truly good in your life? What actions did you see that helped you know that?

_____

_____

In your own life, how have you taught others about goodness?

_____

_____

### Ideas for Demonstrating Goodness

- ☐ Speak and act with integrity.
- ☐ Be an example for others in the community and church.
- ☐ Look for those who are downtrodden, neglected, and vulnerable, and stand up for them.
- ☐ Don't worry about what is politically correct; do what is right in God's eyes.

## Great Is Thy Faithfulness

### 2 Corinthian 5:7, Ephesians 3:16–17

They stood, facing each other in a gazebo, encircled by flowers and friends. Joining hands, they pledged their love to one another, each speaking the sentence: "I will be faithful to you, forsaking all others, till death do we part." Faithful, each committing to the other, promising to always be there, to put that person first, to have no others before their loved one, to find joy in one another, laugh together, cry together.

God asks us, as Christians, to be faithful to Him, and He has modeled what that looks like by how He treats us. He is the only one who has been faithful to each of us, no matter what, from the lowest lows to the most joyful highs and all the days in between, from the day of our birth to forever. His faithfulness to us is the one constant in our lives. As humans, we try hard to live out that word "faithful" in our relationships with others, but only our Lord displays pure, unblemished faithfulness.

And to whom should I pledge my faith? Who should I keep my eyes on?

After my dad passed away, I remember meeting with our minister and saying, "I lost my rock when my dad died." She looked at me and gently asked, "Who should be your rock, Kathy?"

There was a pause as God's love washed over me and awareness filled me: "God."

God is our rock and is ever faithful to us, and it is God, regardless of life events and circumstances, that we need to put our faith in. He won't leave, He never dies, He doesn't forsake us. All we have to do is say, "God," and He is there, or if our pain is such that we can't even say the word, He is already there.

In living these attributes, God is asking each of us to demonstrate faithfulness in our own daily lives, faithfulness to Him and faithfulness to each other and our ministry for Him. He is asking us to be there, be there in ministry, in love. Be there whole-heartedly, dedicated to Him, for others. He is asking that we display character in our lives and be someone who is tried and true for others, displaying a deep and abiding faith in God, living out the fruit, the attributes of being a Christian.

## Reflection

Share a time in your past when someone was faithful to you.

_____

_____

When did you show faithfulness?

_____

_____

### Ideas for Demonstrating Faithfulness

- ☐ Live in accordance to God's directives in the Bible.
- ☐ Communicate with God every day.
- ☐ Work to discern His will for you.
- ☐ Worship and praise Him.
- ☐ Be there for others consistently.
- ☐ Forgive others and ask God to forgive you.

## Gentle on My Mind

### Ephesians 4:2

What do you see when you hear the word "gentleness"? Are you holding a newborn, your fingers trailing over the softness of their face, your arms holding this precious blanket-wrapped gift of new life, your smile coming almost unbidden to your lips and eyes, your heart gentled by the love, the agape love, that fills you? Do you see a place in God's natural world, maybe by the seashore, with the water lapping gently onto the shore, rolling a shell or two in and out, shore birds gently circling about, the sun slanting, fluffy white clouds making the blue sky seem even brighter?

Who do you see yourself with when you consider gentleness? Who is gentle with you? Who brings out gentleness in you? Who slows you down, gives you time to consider what matters in your life? Where are you? What vision fills your eyes, all your senses, bringing a deep peace and gentleness to you? What might you be doing that is reflective and calming? Is gentleness something that comes to us, something that we search out, something that is just a part of how we approach life? These are questions to consider as we each search for the part gentleness plays in our lives.

There are times when gentleness has been compared to meekness, but that is not true. Gentleness is strength, is choosing to remain calm and reflective, choosing to have a tranquil spirit and to carefully consider options and one's responses to others. It is not being proud or boastful; it is taking the time to maintain a balance and completeness of one's own life before interacting and becoming a part of another's life. Gentleness is shown to us by God. He is constant, stable, kind, careful, amazing power under control, surrounded by gentleness; be gentle.

## Reflection

Who has shown you gentleness? How have they shown it?

_____

_____

When is a time being gentle helped you face a circumstance in your life, helped you be there to help another person?

_____

_____

### Ideas for Demonstrating Gentleness

- ☐ Be kind.
- ☐ Be patient.
- ☐ Show love.
- ☐ Be calm.
- ☐ Show self-control.
- ☐ Color your attitude in a positive way,
- ☐ Show your love through your actions.

## Can't Take My Eyes Off of You: Self-Control

### 2 Peter 1:5–8

The problem actually started at the grocery store. I accidentally turned down the chips aisle, and then … I kept going. Oh my; all those bags of chips were calling to me, "Put me in your cart." I was salivating. I almost made it when my eyes spied the barbecue kettle chips, and I knew I was done in. My grip became sweaty; I tried to turn my head, but rationalizing started: "It's just a small bag. I'll share them with Tom. The kids are coming in a few days. I'll have a couple now and save them for the kids." Into the cart went the kettle chips; into the cupboard they went when I got home, but by the time I had put away all the groceries, the chips were back out on the counter, open and half-gone. Don't ask me if Tom got any of them or if there were any left by bedtime; you can guess that answer. Self-control: not that day, not me.

Self-control is being able to deny yourself, say no and mean it, and follow through on it. It is being master of your actions, your thoughts, your earthly desires. The times when you lose self-control are when impulsivity takes over, when your earthly desires take over, your common sense flees, when what you know is best for you takes a back seat to what makes you feel good or what you want, right now. Questions to ask in those moments are: "What's best for me, for others, in this situation? How does doing this, thinking this, feeling this, acting on this make me a better person and life better for someone else? How does God feel about this?"

I was a bit of an impulsive little girl, a bit hyperactive, and I think my folks always worried about self-control with me, because they talked about it a lot. I remember my dad saying to me often, "Most things in life are fine, in moderation. It's when they become excessive and you can't stop yourself from doing, saying, being, that they become wrong." I can still hear his voice, even in the chips aisle.

The biggest question of all is, "Who is in control?" Do chips control me, or do I control the chips? Have I asked God to help me with times I struggle with self-control? Chips are small potatoes in life (pun intended). There are much bigger issues that you need to give God control of, such as what you choose to say to others, the way you spend your time, relationship decisions, how to respond to someone who has hurt you, choosing whether to worry over something you have no control over, choosing to focus on aches and pains and forgetting to really live, choosing to focus on what is wrong in your life and not paying attention to the blessings, and more.

God is there. God wants to be in control. God wants to lift all of this from your shoulders, to help you carry it, to carry you. Exercise your self-control; put the reins on, pull back on them sometimes, let God hold the reins, steer, guide. The barn is ahead, and He'll get you safely there. Hmmm, wonder if there are chips in the barn; just wondering.

## Reflection

What is an area in your life where you struggle with self-control?

_____

_____

How can your relationship with God help you practice self-control?

_____

_____

**Ideas for Demonstrating Self-Control**

- ☐ Show control over health issues.
- ☐ Temper what you say to others.
- ☐ Take concerns to God in prayer; let Him help you.
- ☐ Wait before you react.
- ☐ Be patient.
- ☐ Exercise and make wise food choices.
- ☐ Be aware of the messages of your body language.

## Action Item

Identify someone you would like to show more of a specific fruit of the Spirit toward. Make a plan with specific actions you will take. Take action.

## My Prayer

Lord,

You have given me Your great love and shown me unconditional love by giving up Your Son. Your greatest commandment for me is to love You and to love my neighbors as myself. The Bible gives me the fruit of the Spirit, which come out of that love. They help me build strong relationships with others. Please help me weave these characteristics into my life. This is how I can show my faith in Jesus. Please guide me in awareness of the fruit of the Spirit as I leave this chapter. Help me share love with others I meet.

In Jesus's name,

Amen

## Chapter 5

# Finding Contentment; Bloom Where You're Planted

I am not saying this because I am in need, for I have learned to be content with whatever the circumstances. I know what it is to be in need, and I know what it is to have plenty. I have learned the secret of being content in any and every situation, whether well fed or hungry, whether living in plenty or want. I can do all this through Him who gives me strength.

—Philippians 4:11–13

## Bloom

The colors are parading, flowers blooming in planters on our deck, in the yard, all blooming where they are planted, all loving where they reside, rich soil, enough sunlight, protected from the winds by the house and the woods, fertilized on occasion; nothing can stop this profusion of riotous color. Nothing can stop any of them from blooming where they are planted. It's easy, it's expected, it's part of the summer season here in Michigan.

Change your view to Hawaii, standing on the barren wasteland on the top of the volcano on the big island of Hawaii. In every direction, it is shades of black and gray, with rivers of molten rock frozen into place. The vistas are barren, and the wind is whipping across the rise of the hardened evidence of the earth turned inside out. And then I saw it. Off to my left, in the midst of all that gray and black, was a speck of yellow, standing out in stark relief against the sea of nothingness. I hurried over to it, and as I drew nearer, I realized it was a flower, one brave yellow flower, standing proudly on its stem, blooming despite everything around it giving the message that this was no good place for a plant, a flower, for blooming. It was a flower determined to bloom where it was planted in the most difficult, unexpected place. Yes, it was blooming, and in doing so, it delighted and inspired the eyes that were trained on it.

This chapter will help us consider a variety of circumstances in our lives and how to live above the circumstances, to find contentment through our Lord, regardless of what life hands to us, to bloom where we are planted.

## When the Soil Is Good and When the Soil Is Not

"Bloom where you are planted" has a happy lilt to it, and when life is good, when the soil is good, much like my backyard right now, it is just a happy concept to consider. When you have a happy marriage, a good relationship with your spouse, it's not hard to be happy, productive, and positive. When you have friendly, kind neighbors, it's easy to be a good neighbor. When your job is one you wanted, that you enjoy, and the people around you are good, responsible, and upbeat, it's not so hard to be blooming on that job. When not only your basic needs are met, but also lots of those wants too, it's not hard to be the showy flower, blooming vibrantly and vigorously where you are planted.

The much greater challenge is when we find ourselves in situations that are hard, that we didn't choose, or that, if we did choose, ended up extremely difficult, hard to manage, hard to live with. There are instances such as a broken relationship between a husband and a wife, a willful child or one with a debilitating illness, a job that you took only because you couldn't find any other and you had to meet your family's needs. These situations are very difficult to deal with.

As humans, we get planted for many years in one type of soil, and then life can change, gradually or in a heartbeat. I think about how I enjoyed being a mom, but then one day, they all grew up; my role as a daily, involved, caring mother ended, and it hurt. I remember watching my son marry, so hopeful that he would have a happy life and family, but after painful years and their divorce, that dream is dead. I remember my difficult miscarriages, Tom's debilitating depression, the deaths of our parents, and more. I didn't sign up for those, didn't want those, and I remember that blooming looked almost impossible to me.

We cannot control the cards we are dealt, but we can control how we play them. Sometimes, when we play euchre with friends, I'll pick up my five cards, and there will be two black or two red jacks (if you play euchre, you'll know those are very good cards to find). In addition, there may be aces, or you might see all the cards in one suit. I have to work hard to keep that poker face. I know it's going to be easy to play these cards, and it's going to be fun. On other hands, I may find all nines and tens and varied suits. These are not good at all. But if those nines and tens are in trump, there's a possibility that with my partner's cards, we can set the other players, so we play carefully. We choose how to play them.

That's life, isn't it? We can't always choose the situations. I didn't choose my miscarriages or my parents' illnesses or my son's divorce, but I did have a choice in how I handled those situations. It is normal and healthy to let emotions out; I was sad and, yes, angry about losing my babies. I was overwhelmed and ran the gamut of emotions with my parents. I was hurt for my son. I could choose to stay stuck in those emotions or to work them through, let go and move ahead, go on to bloom. I chose how to play those cards.

Can we be like the seed of the yellow flower on the volcano: sometimes carried on the wind, sometimes planted in places we would never choose, places that aren't particularly conducive to our health and growth, and still look for what is good, still grow, and still bloom? If we are open and aware, if we trust our Lord, the answer is yes. We can choose, when we land in difficult spots, to grow or to not grow. We can choose in those situations to be bitter or to be better.

I think back to my dad's childhood as an example of this. His parents divorced when he was twelve. Last summer, I received a packet with his parents' divorce records. In the packet was a four-page letter his dad had written to his mom's parents, detailing the difficulties in the marriage, that my dad's mother had gone off with another man, and that now his dad was living with another woman. This was a village of about five hundred people, with my dad on the cusp of being a teenager. I can only imagine the emotional turmoil he lived through; he is a prime example of someone having to choose: Will I be better because of this, or will I be bitter? Will I live my life determined to make the best of it, have a good marriage, be a good dad, do a good job, contribute to others, or will I be angry, destructive, and abusive? I am so thankful he chose to be better.

## Reflection

Was there a time in your life when it was easy to bloom? Was there a time in your life when it was difficult to bloom?

_____

_____

*Kathy Herrick*

# Life Lessons

"I have come that they may have life, and have it to the full" (John 10:10).

I took my first step across the threshold of formalized education at the age of four and stepped away from it at age twenty, newly earned diploma in my hand, heading out to realize a lifelong dream of being a teacher. I thought I knew it all, but then the real education began.

I arrived at an elementary school that suddenly needed more teachers, as the local Catholic school had suddenly closed, and scores of new students would now be coming there. I was hired to teach language arts in a departmentalized setting to fifth and sixth graders. I was excited, until I walked into the room I had been assigned, to find absolutely nothing beyond desks, chairs, and an old chicken bone under the sink. Nothing; my heart sank, and the lessons began: life lessons.

Disappointment, life not living up to expectations, frustration. I had a choice: bitter or better. I went home and started writing curriculum, writing stories for the kids to read, ordered materials with my own money, created bulletin boards, begged the secretary (the principal had left) for art supplies, and we were off and running. I learned about curriculum structure from the ground up. I learned about my own gifts and talents, both those I had and those I did not. I learned to search out those who could support both the teacher and her students. Life lessons.

Then the students arrived: classes of over thirty, six a day, rotating around, all ten- and eleven-year-olds, and many who had had the thumb of nuns on them for years. And here I was, twenty years old, green, nervous, unsure … and they knew it. They went in for the kill, with behavior sure to shock and destroy any young teacher. Another life lesson was in process. Hmmm: bitter or better. I chose the backbone, deciding it was me or them, and it wasn't going to be me. In reality, I learned about human nature, learned to love my students and build relationships, learned about respect built on that, learned that bringing them into the process of responsibility for their own behavior would change everything. Life lessons.

So many times, we hit some really tough bumps in life, and in the moments of those bumps, it hurts. It is hard; we are overcome. We would do anything to push them away. But in reality, many of those moments teach us more about how to do life and about ourselves as individuals and as members of God's family, of our family, of society, and of the world, than in any other manner. I had to dig deep to learn to be a good teacher, to learn about relationships. I never forgot those lessons. They have been a part of me over the years, as an educator, family member, friend, church member, and more.

I believe now that in each of the bumps we face in life, God is teaching us, preparing us, for something to come in our lives; we are enduring the tough soil, the winds, the drought, the sunless moments to prepare us for the opportunity to bloom as we minister to others. They prepare us to understand others, to relate to where they are, to help them grow and learn. They prepare us to connect, love, encourage, mentor. and inspire.

Those moments of not blooming, not growing, remind me of the tulip bulbs that lie dormant all winter here in Holland, Michigan. Have you ever really examined a tulip bulb? Pretty ugly. They look utterly useless. And yet, after they have been buried in the soil, after a winter of no sun, no rain, no growth, they push forward in the spring to bring forth amazingly beautiful flowers. Tulips in Michigan mean Tulip Time: a festival and a riot of color, all because these ugly bulbs rested, gathered strength, prepared for what was next.

Life is like that too; there are times when we must rest, germinate, study, speculate, take time off, to get ready to learn, pray, plan, gather strength for what is next: for those blooming moments.

## Reflection

What are some lessons you have learned through life experiences?

_____

_____

## Deciding to Bloom; Being Content

When life hands you lemons, make lemonade. When life hands you tough situations, make the best of it. When the soil looks bad, haul in some new dirt; when the sun is blocked, trim back the trees; when there's a drought, haul water from a river. Make the most of the experiences in your life, whether they are a challenge or a joy. Put your energy into finding blessings and joy in every circumstance: the silver linings. God can help you find that abundance, He can help you create a new norm. Build your relationships with others; take care of yourself and give yourself time to heal, to reach out to others. Don't sit back and wait; follow your passions and interests. Be yourself; love, love, love, serve others, and bloom. Bloom with the beauty that is yours alone, that has been uniquely given to you by God; bloom with the fragrance of the Lord.

We can choose to live above the circumstances, to focus on Christ and the positive instead of the negative. We can choose to get up, and as hard as it is, to move, to slowly slide one foot in front of the other one, with His help. I don't believe for minute that God causes bad things to happen, but I do believe He is there to help us go through them, to give us support and strength through those circumstances.

## Reflection

What are some blessings you see in a difficult situation you have had?

_____

_____

What are ways to take care of yourself spiritually, physically, mentally, and emotionally, ways to build contentment?

_____

_____

## Getting Rid of the Weeds

I just got back from a walk down the street, and the house two doors down, oh my! The front yard is full of weeds, a yard they just redid a few years ago. The weeds are choking out all of the beautiful flowers and bushes they planted. Someone needs to tend to that yard, to those beds.

We are like that too; if we don't manage our lives, seek to stay away from sin (weeds), they can take over, can choke out what is good in our lives. Sometimes, they may not seem like bad things; consider the computer that I am busy typing on. It's a great tool. I can find information I need, communicate with people, work on this book. But what if I let it steal all of my time? What if I spend all day playing games on it, checking for email, scanning social media, and neglect caring for myself, my family, and following pursuits I say matter to me. There are times that weeds look innocent and simple, but we must be thoughtful and meet the challenges head on.

Weeds can also be self-defeating behaviors, and it's important that we ask God to help us be aware of our own attitudes and behaviors and how to take on a more hopeful, positive approach, and help us be a more kind and caring friend for others.

Sometimes, when trying to manage something differently, it can help to have a friend aware of that, to hold you accountable. I make decisions in my mind; I can pray about them, but if I verbalize them to someone who cares about me, and they come asking, "So how are you doing with that?" it keeps me more focused. Consider all the New Year's resolutions that never make it past January 1. Weeding is not easy.

## Reflection

What do I need to "weed" out of my life?

_____

_____

What is a strategy I will use to manage the "weeds"?

_____

_____

## Bloom

Bloom; share your beauty with all.
Bloom; spread God's fragrance.
Bloom; as God's dear child.
Bloom; His story you'll tell.

## Strategies to Help Us Keep Blooming

- ☐ Regardless of what others are doing around you, bloom.
- ☐ Don't expect others to change; you can control yourself, not them.
- ☐ Stay peaceful, tranquil, even when others aren't.
- ☐ Persevere.
- ☐ Your life today connects to your future life; be deliberate about where and how.
- ☐ Look for a higher purpose.
- ☐ Do your best.
- ☐ Regardless of where you are planted, look for that crack, a place to grow.
- ☐ Take advantage of opportunities.
- ☐ Appreciate where and how you live.
- ☐ Set goals and keep track of them.
- ☐ Go with the flow.
- ☐ Spend your time with family and friends.
- ☐ Balance your life.
- ☐ Be friendly and open with others.
- ☐ Accept what you can't change; change what you can.
- ☐ Have a positive outlook.
- ☐ Be active in your community and church.
- ☐ Be thankful for what you have.

The only attitude you can control is your own.

## Action Item

List areas of your life that matter. Consider how much time you spend in each area. Choose one to spend more time on and one to spend less time on. Act on those choices.

*Kathy Herrick*

## My Prayer

Lord,

In my life, I have faced many circumstances that have either brought me down or raise me up. I've had tough bumps that make me feel alone and smooth places where I coast along without worry. I am now taking a serious look at myself. I ask You, "Where am I headed?" I can be bitter or better. I can study, pray, plan, gather strength, and finally bloom where I am. I can learn about myself and where I fit as an individual in a community and as a member of God's family. As I work on my new commission, please guide me. Help me keep out the weeds that might cause me to stray from the life you have in store for me.

In Jesus's name,

Amen

# Chapter 6

## Heart-to-Heart Friends; Friends in Christ

A friend loves you all the time. A brother is always there to help you.
—Proverbs 17:17

## Friends

No written contract or rules, no signatures on legal documents are required to be a friend. We choose our friends and the kind of friend we are. We choose how much effort we put into the relationship. Friends, a valuable commodity, take away loneliness, shelter us with care, surround us with love, help us know we have a place of importance in this very big world, a place by their side and under their wings.

One of our basic human needs is to connect with others on a deeper level, to feel love, to have friends. We crave having a sense of belonging, and we want to know that no matter what life hands us, our friends will be there. Sharing the love of God deepens those friendships. God works through people; He created friendships as a way for us to minister to each other.

"Friends are angels who lift us to our feet when our wings have trouble remembering how to fly." (Unknown).

Sayings about friendship can be found everywhere. As you shop, look around, and you will find friendship sayings on plaques, mugs, journals, posters, and more. Everyone has thoughts about friendship, about what makes a good friend, and what friendship means in our lives. So let's spend time together considering what friendship, friends with Christ, friends through Christ, and friends in Christ really means. We'll be discovering what our Lord tells us about making new friends, about being a friend, and about what causes stumbling blocks to friendship.

## Reflection

What makes someone a good friend? What would you say is true friendship?

_____

_____

## Making New Friends; Loneliness

When you don't have the close fellowship of friends, the emotions associated with loneliness can become the mantle you wear. Loneliness can be prevalent when you move from a place of many friends to a place of few or none. It can also be found as you move into new stages of life; as you age, close friends may become ill or pass away. You miss the confidence of knowing you have that special person to talk to, do things with, who always cares about you. Loneliness can become pervasive; if not addressed, it can become a self-fulfilling condition of emptiness and negativity.

Finding and making new friends is an active proposition. You cannot sit back and wait for it to happen, because in many cases, it won't. You have to step out of your comfort zone and be willing to feel a little uncomfortable, timid, insecure, shy. Make yourself step right over those feelings and connect with others. You have to keep firmly in mind that God is always walking with you, even as you meet and get to know new friends.

Pray, reach out, pray some more, take time, make plans, take God along with you, and make connections with new friends. Where can you look for new friends? Try taking a class; you will find those who share that interest with you. How about joining a club? There will be a commonality that brings you both to that club. In our neighborhood, we have a book club, card clubs, golf groups, and a knitting group: places where you will find friendly people who also enjoy those activities.

Another place to find new friends, especially heart-to-heart friends, is at church. But if your church is like ours, big, if you want to make friends, you can't just walk in, sit down for the service, and walk out, expecting others to come up and make connections. You have to take responsibility for the friend search. Sign up for a class, go to a Sunday school class, volunteer for a mission activity, join a musical group. All of these will bring you into smaller groups with more opportunities to connect and get to know each other.

## Reflection

List some ways you can make new friends.

_____

_____

In what ways can you combat your own loneliness or that of others?

_____

_____

## Being a Good Friend; God's Instructions

### Love
### Proverbs 17:17, John 13:34–35

How does God define friendship? Love … that's it! It is sharing and being open, being there, caring so much that the heart squeezes a bit. Love: friendship, modeled by God and given to us as a gift, friendship with God, friendship with each other. We may not share the same DNA as our friends, may not have fought over who was straying over that imaginary line in the back of our '55 Chevy, as I did with my sister, but our Christian friends share the love of our Lord. Through that love, we quickly become heart-to-heart friends: loving, trusting, supporting.

At a meeting recently, someone commented, "I have enough friends." Do we ever have enough friends? What is God's model for us? He never has enough children, and He's provided a whole wide world of possible friends out there for us, just waiting for our friendship. He asks us to meet, greet, and get to know each other, offering the hand of friendship. He asks us to not pull that hand back, but to let our hands lie together, explore what is the same about us, and celebrate what is different.

So step out of your comfort zone, the circle of your current friends, and take on the challenge of befriending someone new. God has blessings awaiting you, through new friends.

## Reflection

Who is someone you have recently met that you can nurture as a friend? How will you do that?

_____

_____

## Encourage Each Other

### Hebrews 10:24–25

As friends, encourage each other. Look back and identify times when your friends were your cheerleaders, your encouragers, when they helped you get through difficult times. One way God ministers to us is through Christian friends; we can see the hand of God in their support. Our friends can help us sort out thoughts and feelings, help us make big decisions, and encourage us to keep going in difficult times.

A few years ago, my mom broke her hip, and as I dealt with it in Michigan, I felt pretty much alone. Then came a short email from a friend in Florida: "You're not alone, we're with you in spirit." When I wasn't sure about teaching after my challenging first year, a friend boosted me up and reminded me of the skills she saw in me. When I wasn't sure about being a good enough writer to share a daily Bible study, friends encouraged me to give it a try. Friends can see our spiritual gifts and encourage us to find ways to use them. And most importantly: God is the greatest encourager of all.

Have we encouraged others? Is encouragement something that is just there for others to do for us, or do we provide encouragement for our friends? Do we look for ways that we can help them face life, step out in service, use their gifts? Think about your friends, their encouragement of you, and your encouragement of them. Find someone new to encourage today, find ways to help them open up, let out God's love and light, serve others. I encourage you to do this.

## Reflection

Who is someone you can encourage today? What is one way you can encourage them?

_____

_____

## Be There

### Hebrews 13:5

God gives us what we need; there are times in our lives when we need our friends and times when they need us. When I was afraid to walk into Sunday school as a little one, there was Mary, slipping her hand into mine. When I was nervous about being our church youth group president, there was Janet, eagerly joining in the planning. As I struggled with nerves about whether I could work as a teacher and be a mom too, there was Joanie, telling me I could. As I was nervously starting the first session as a leader of a class at church, there was Phyllis, smiling, and telling me with that smile, I could do it. Think back and remember when your friends have been there for you. Thank God, and think about when you've been there for others; think about when God has been there for you.

When we are friends in our Lord, our bonds are strong and true. When we are friends with our Lord, we know that He will help guide our daily walk. In all cases, friends are there: to help with the nerves and the confidence, the belief in ourselves, to pick us up, set us down, move in front of us, stand beside us, pick up the load with us (or for us), stand behind us. Friends, our Christian friends, our Lord, are there with whatever we need, but most importantly, they are there.

Let us each look for ways to be there for each other, to be there for God.

## Reflection

When was a friend there for you? When were you there for a friend?

_____

_____

## Have Fun

### Psalm 126:2

Tom and our boys are known for belly laughs. I think it's in their DNA. They're not laughing all the time, but when something really tickles them, that laughter comes rolling out from deep in their bellies. It's so funny; while the original thing might not make me laugh, those belly laughs do.

Laughter, joy, happiness, smiling, having fun: God wants all of that for us, with our friends and our families. Scripture tells us to be filled with laughter, not to just snicker, but to be so tickled by something that laughter just rolls out, rises right up out of our bellies. God wants us to enjoy our friends, to plan and have happy times together, to recognize that those wonderful moments are indeed blessings He sends to us.

Stand in front of a mirror, watch your face, give a giggle, think of something silly, giggle a little more, take a deep breath right down to your belly, and give a big belly laugh. There you go; doesn't that feel great? Next, make a connection with a friend, share a funny time together, laugh. Laughter with friends lets them know you believe they are a joy to be with; it's a friendship to be valued. Go ahead, don't squelch down those belly laughs. I mean, after all, God tells you to be filled with laughter; go for it.

## Reflection

When you look back, when is a time you remember laughing out loud with a friend? How can using humor help in making new friends?

_____

_____

## Inspiration

### 2 Timothy 3:16–17

He sat on the chair, a little boy, with feet dangling. His eyes were intent on the paper he held, which was covered with the loops and sticks of his own handwriting. In front of him, on the rug, sat twenty of his peers, leaning forward. He began to read. A flying saucer approached the earth, hovered, and then landed in his own backyard. Little green men with box-like heads, arms and legs like springs, making noises like the beeping of the dishwasher when it is done, came out, and on the story went. When he finished, the children clapped and wildly waved their hands. Calling on them, he learned they loved his story. A few gave him ideas for his next story, and they begged him to make it into a book so that they could read it again.

He slid off the big chair; looking at me, he said, "Mrs. Herrick, I must get back to work and get this story into a book because I have lots of new ideas percolating in my brain." Great kid; a great example of what kind of inspiration our friends can be.

Friends can cheer for what we've done today; they can help us see how we can take the gift and extend it, turn it into something that goes on and makes a difference for even more people. They can also inspire us to start anew and keep going, keep giving, keep living a life for God.

Inspiration: God sends it to us through His word, His whispers, nature, our friends' appreciation and encouragement … and yes, through their ideas added to ours, which can lead to amazing ideas. Be open to their inspiration and to God's; be willing to inspire others. It's called friendship.

## Reflection

When have you been inspired by someone else? When have you felt inspired by God? As you look ahead, how might you inspire someone else?

_____

_____

## Accepting

### Romans 14:1, Romans 15:7

Acceptance: Scripture is clear; just because you don't share my opinions is no reason not to draw you in close as my friend, as a member of my group. We are told to accept others, to not turn our backs on them, to not argue or shun them for their opinions. In arguments, not discussions, there is distancing; there is separation. How do we reach others if we are not open, accepting, loving, willing to share our views, opinions, ideas, but also willing to listen to their views, opinions, and ideas?

Christ accepts us, as imperfect as we are, and asks us to accept each other. Consider how Jesus accepts you; then as you are given opportunities to meet new folks and make friends, reach out and make the most of these opportunities. How will you show the love of our Lord? How will you help others be ready to learn about that love?

## Reflection

How can you show an openness and acceptance to friends?

_____

_____

*Kathy Herrick*

## Being God's Letter

### 2 Corinthians 3:1–3

We are the letter from Christ. My entire life, I've gotten so excited when a letter comes addressed to me in the snail mail. As a little girl, I would run to open the mailbox and pull out the mail, hoping to see "Miss Kathy Richards" on the envelope. Usually those were from Gramma, but as I got older, they might have been from a new camp friend or even later from a boyfriend. Later, as a wife and mom, the letters I craved were from my mother and from childhood and college friends (before the days of email). Now I still love to have that letter from a loved one in my hand.

But how does God send letters to us, here on earth? How do His messages get passed from one person to another, from friend to friend? We have no metal mailbox that says, "From Heaven." He doesn't use paper and pencil, the US Post Office, or a computer, but He does send out mail.

We are the letters that God writes. People watch us and read us. People understand what being a Christian means and what being a friend is all about by looking at our lives. We are God's paper and pencil, and the words flow from us. As we share words of encouragement, we are His letters. As we greet new people and begin to become friends, we are His letters. As we accept others, even when they are different from us, we are His letters. As we pray for each other, study the Bible, yes, even share a casserole, we are His letters. His letters include sharing His good news, loving one another, and supporting His work in and through each of His children.

Let's commit to letter writing and live our lives so that others are reading of God's love and light, every day, through us.

## Reflection

What message from God are you "writing" to others?

_____

_____

## Forgiveness

### Matthew 6:14–15, 18:21–22

Forgiving friends and loved ones who hurt you, letting it go, showing grace, mending fences that thoughtless actions and words can bring about is hard. Can you look back over your life and see where forgiveness has kept a friend close or lack of forgiveness has meant a broken relationship? They are there: the friendships that have grown through tending and lost relationships that happen when pride stands in the way.

I believe the hardest friendships for me have been those people who believe they have done nothing wrong, have not hurt me, or have not done something that was unkind or uncaring, and yet I've been hurt by their actions (or lack of action). How do you forgive someone who doesn't even see a need to be forgiven?

It took me a very long time to realize that God does not ask the other person to ask us to forgive them, but rather He asks us to just forgive that person ourselves, wipe off that hurt, anger, and sorrow, and hand the relationship to Him. If we can forgive and let it go, it frees us, heals our hearts, and perhaps over time, the other person will see the difference in us (but perhaps not). I don't believe God asks us to forget, but I do believe He asks us to forgive and to not let our own hearts be all twisted in anger and hurt. He asks us to show grace to others as He shows grace to us. I also believe it means we don't keep putting ourselves in a position to be hurt over and over, if possible.

Forgiveness between Christian friends goes both ways. We've been looking at forgiving others, the action we can take, but God also asks us to be willing to ask others to forgive us. I don't believe any of us purposefully hurts others, but it happens. If it has happened to you, put pride in the back seat and be willing to ask for forgiveness. Look for ways to help others feel better and show them you value their friendship.

Forgiveness: Jesus is the most amazing example of that. He forgives us for everything, over and over again. It's not easy to forgive. Hurt and anger can sit deep in our souls; I think "evil" likes to keep stirring them sometimes, but God asks us to exert our free will to forgive and to ask for forgiveness. True friendship is not always perfect or easy. Hard bumps happen and will happen again. But what is important is that we let the bonds of friendship be stronger than that, for our Jesus is stronger than any bump. Forgive.

## Reflection

When is a time you have asked a friend to forgive you? When is a time you have forgiven a friend? Is there something in your life right now that you need to examine or need to forgive someone for? Is there something you need to ask forgiveness for?

_____

_____

## Trustworthy

### 1 Corinthians 1:9

"I've got your back." When you walked into a new class and saw your friend, stress drained out of your body. When you saw a group of bullies ahead but knew your friend was beside you, your head stayed up. In each case, you knew you could trust your friend to stand beside you.

Trust is precious, given in love, maintained through consistently showing each other it is real, and letting our friends know they are safe with us. And the other side of the coin is always knowing we are safe with them. We have to be vulnerable ourselves; open ourselves to our Christian friends; be willing to let them see our hearts, our joys, and our sorrows, our vulnerabilities and our strengths, our wants and our gifts; be willing to trust that what they say and do is done in love; and be willing to trust. God gives us the most amazing Christian friendships when we let go of self, trust them, and let them trust us, just as we can always trust God.

## Reflection

Where have you seen trust at work in a friendship you have with someone?

_____

_____

## Being a Friend When It Is Hard

### Galatians 6:1–6

If we see a brother or sister wandering away, we aren't to just let them go. We are to leave behind our comfortable, often complacent spot and forge out into the wild to tap them on the shoulder and say, "Hey, wait a minute; can I help you find your way back onto the path and back into the fold? I'll be here. I'll help you. I'll hold your hand. You have to take the first step back in that direction, but I'll be right beside you. I promise, I won't leave you." And this is what Jesus does for us.

Help others with troubles; don't judge. Be responsible for yourself. Scripture tells us we should help our fellow Christians when they need to make something right. We are not to shun that person but are to forgive them as God has, help them make it right, and support them as they make new choices and travel a new path—God's path.

Our role is often to model right living; be kind; treat and love others as God does; keep doors open, ears at the ready, and minds open and accepting; ask the right questions; point out consequences; offer options; give companionship; study with them; live a real life for God that they can see; and share concern with a loving approach—What Jesus does for us.

It's hard to do, but as you consider what Jesus would do, ask God to help in your interactions and relationships. Picture Jesus by the gate, where the one sheep has wandered away. The rest are safe in the enclosure, but off He goes to find the lost sheep and bring it back into the fold. We are told to do as Jesus did.

## Reflection

When was a time it was hard to help a friend?

_____

_____

## Stumbling Blocks to Friendship

Friendship: The word is a happy one; the thoughts of sharing great times with friends make us smile, but in reality, being a good friend—a good Christian friend—takes work. Some human tendencies can get in the way of friendship and cause good friends to stumble, and unless both are acutely aware of these possibilities, they may even drive friends apart. Below is a list of possible stumbling blocks and ways, with God's help, we can overcome them.

**Accusing:** No matter what others say, follow Jesus's example: be quiet and don't respond.
**Arguing:** No one wins in arguments; small ones can become big ones. Don't start an argument, and don't add to it; be the one to walk away. Arguments are not discussions.
**Betraying:** Be true to God and to your friends.
**Complaining:** Don't complain; look for the positive, for the blessings. Do His work and help friends cheerfully.
**Gossiping:** Don't start it, don't participate in it; build up people and recognize that each person is God's child. We are all special.
**Being Greedy:** Remember everything belongs to God. Be content with what you have, recognize when you have all you need, and be a giving person.
**Being Jealous:** Be satisfied with God's blessings for you. Let God know you are thankful for what you have. Practice happiness for others.
**Lying:** Be honest. Don't tell a small lie; it can lead to large ones. Don't think you can hide truth in your life; God knows all. Ask God and friends for forgiveness.

Work to keep your heart and mind free of these stumbling blocks, with God's help. Let love be your motivator and your basis for your friendships.

## Action Item

Identify someone you want to strengthen your friendship with. List specific ways you will do that. Choose one way and take action.

## My Prayer

Lord, Master, and Friend,

Thank You for being my friend and for providing Christian friends in my life to share love with. Your gift of friends provides me with care, compassion, love, and a sense of belonging. Your plan is to teach me to minister to others the way Jesus loves and ministers to me. I have to step out of my comfort zone to be able to connect with others, and I know You will always be with me when I take that unsure step. Please help me to share and to be loving, trusting, supportive, and encouraging of others. I should always be on the lookout for a new friend; I never know when I might touch a heart, and both of us will be rewarded by that friendship. Please help me rejoice in every friend and be open to their counsel and inspiration. I need to accept others and love them for who they are: a child of God, just like me. I am Your mirror for love. Other people will see me as a reflection of Jesus, if I live by loving You. Thank You for the friends you have sent into my life and the ones you are preparing to be my friends. Thank You for giving me the opportunity to take Jesus into the world wherever I go.

In Jesus's name,

Amen

Chapter 7

# Spiritual Gifts; Unwrapping Our Gifts from God

There are different kinds of gifts; but the same Spirit distributes them. There are different kinds of service, but the same Lord. There are different kinds of working, but in all of them and in everyone it is the same God at work. Now to each one the manifestation of the Spirit is given for the common good.

—1 Corinthians 12:4–5

## God's Gifts

Peeking into the living room, I saw packages glittering under the Christmas tree. When I crawled under to peek at a tag, I was thrilled when I saw my name on it. A gift for me, just me—not my sister and me together. God too, has gifts for us, gifts with our individual name written on them.

The greatest gift from God is the gift of Jesus Christ: His life, death, resurrection, and our salvation through Him. He gifts us with blessings and with His forgiveness, mercy, grace, and peace. He offers us life everlasting. There is nothing we pay for this gift, nothing we do to earn it; it is ours because God loves us. Amazing love, amazing grace.

But God also sends along gifts with just your name on the tag. He asks you to reach out, take the gift, and open it. There, you will find spiritual gifts He has chosen uniquely for you, gifts that He knows you need in order to serve Him by serving others.

For God's light, love, and vision to be carried forward to the world and across the generations, He knew He needed the commitment and work of His family. He also knew that it was no small task ahead and that all hands were going to be needed, doing all kinds of jobs. Just as with the human body—different parts with a variety of functions working together to keep us healthy—God needs different individuals within the body of Christ to take on different tasks for His ministry to be successful. And so, He gifted us uniquely. He did not give the same gift to all people, and He gave at least one gift to each person. "I don't have a gift" won't cut it with God because He knows the gift was given. No one has all the gifts; we need each other for the mission to be successful.

Your spiritual gift is important, critically important. Unwrap it, for a gift left wrapped is useless and gathers dust. Use it. A gift admired but stored away on a shelf is also useless. Unwrap it, examine it, learn about it, pray about using it, and take action. When we all use our gifts in concert with each other, we address the common good and are a part of His message to the world and the saving of others. He needs each of us. He needs all of us.

## Why Use Our Gifts?

When Jesus left the earth, He told His followers that He wasn't really leaving, for a part of Him, the Holy Spirit, would be left with them and be a part of them. The Holy Spirit works in us and through us, and we use our gifts to help express our love of God. When we use our gifts, we find contentment and fulfillment. We feel useful and have a sense of belonging in God's family. God has work for us and asks us to produce fruit. Using our gifts in His service is a part of that, and as we do so, we are obeying Him.

## Scriptural Basis

### Acts 6:1–7

The followers mentioned in these verses were frustrated. Jobs weren't getting done, a few people were trying to do it all, and some may have been doing little or nothing. What did they do? They accepted that different people were good at different things, and they got organized by assigning tasks based on spiritual gifts. People did the work; their ministry was stronger, and more people accepted God.

When we do His work as a group, it can be far more powerful than striking out alone. He reminds us that our gifts are not the same; we are different, and that's a good thing. When a few try to do it all, often nothing gets done, or those few burn out and stop working. We need to look at others, notice their gifts, open the door of service to them, and encourage them. We all need to realize that no matter how small our gifts may seem, they're important to God's mission. Just think what can be done in His name when we all work together.

## Specific Gifts

### Romans 12:1–8, 1 Corinthians 12, 1 Peter 4:10

You will certainly find different lists of gifts; some are spiritual, and others are more like talents, abilities, or something you have learned. Most of us have a good understanding of what our talents are; they usually correspond to the activities, clubs, and other pursuits in our lives. By combining that knowledge with an understanding of what our gifts are, we can have a clearer picture of what purpose God has for us and where He would see our dreams leading us.

The following twelve gifts are listed for you to read about, reflect on, and consider. You will not have all of these gifts, but you do have at least one gift. It's important that we understand all of the gifts God gives and how they may be applied. In the application of our gifts, we need to be in concert together, to complement each other. I need to understand how someone with the gift of hospitality can work together with someone like me, who has a different gift from God, with both of us working toward the same mission outcome.

The following activities are suggestions from groups of women identified as gifted in varied areas through taking a spiritual gifts inventory at one of our women's ministry programs. Together, they brainstormed practical suggestions for the application of their gifts.

## Evangelism

A person with this gift clearly shares God's message, brings others to know and accept Christ, and helps them grow as God's disciples (Matthew 28:16–20).

### Using the Gift of Evangelism

- ☐ Speak with excitement.
- ☐ Join service projects.
- ☐ Listen to motivational speakers with others.
- ☐ Talk about church and God to others.
- ☐ Have God at the center of your life.

☐ Encourage Christian leaders to keep working.

☐ Share information about God's good news so that others may learn.

☐ Motivate others by sharing one's testimony.

☐ Be "high" on Jesus.

## Exhortation

A person with this gift reaches out to believers in love, helps them grow in their relationship with God, and encourages them to discover God's purpose in their lives (3 John 5–6).

### Using the Gift of Exhortation

☐ Encourage others to trust God.

☐ Pray with others.

☐ Be a good role model.

☐ Share godly moments.

☐ Give financially.

☐ Facilitate a Bible study group.

## Faith

People with the gift of faith continually see the Holy Spirit at work and have complete trust in God. They have the confidence that God will guide them and care for them in a future they do not need to know about ahead of time. They do not let the circumstances of their lives change their faith in God (Mark 5:25–34).

### Using the Gift of Faith

☐ Pray.

☐ Share and give testimony.

☐ Encourage others.

☐ Share scripture.

☐ Read books and suggest books to others.

☐ Attend meetings and retreats.

☐ Be a part of a Bible study group.

☐ Live the faith; walk the walk.

☐ Bloom with joy in any situation because of faith and trust in God.

☐ Let go and let God.

☐ Journal and share how faith has helped in difficult times.

☐ Be a blessing and give thanks for all things.

- ☐ Reach out to family.
- ☐ Listen to and obey God's soft whispers.

## Giving

People with this gift give cheerfully and generously of their time, talents, and treasures, without thought of anything in return. They believe all belongs to God and is only on loan to us. They view giving to others as giving to God. They know meeting the basic needs of others is important in God's mission to the world (2 Corinthians 9:6–15).

### Using the Gift of Faith

- ☐ Volunteer in outreach missions.
- ☐ Help with fundraising.
- ☐ Work at a church welcome desk or usher.
- ☐ Help friends dealing with tragedies.
- ☐ Share with others.
- ☐ Open one's home to others.
- ☐ Support the church's missions financially and with time and talents.

## Hospitality

If this is your gift, you cheerfully welcome others, including guests. You help with food, open your home to others, and inspire friendly fellowship. You are welcoming within the church and church family and in varied missions. You model your welcoming spirit on the example of Jesus (Romans 12:13).

### Using the Gift of Hospitality

- ☐ Serve with hospice or other caring missions.
- ☐ Be instrumental in spearheading neighborliness, not only at home, but also at church and in other groups.
- ☐ Work the visitors' desk or be a greeter at church.
- ☐ Invite others to church events.
- ☐ Listen closely to others.
- ☐ Volunteer to be a hostess at various events.

## Knowledge

People with this gift have a thirst for deeper knowledge. They personally study the Bible, analyze it, and look for new insights. They find and share God's truths with others (1 Corinthians 12:8).

### Using the Gift of Knowledge

- ☐ Learn more about different faith beliefs.
- ☐ Combat discrimination and misinformation.
- ☐ Attend Bible studies.
- ☐ Attend disciple classes and other Sunday school classes.
- ☐ Learn about various ministries of the church, both at home and abroad.
- ☐ Travel with a church group to the Holy Land.
- ☐ Join a prayer group.
- ☐ Read a devotional every day.

## Leadership

A person with the gift of Christian leadership, based on a belief in God's word and His guidance, confidently motivates and leads others to follow their dreams and gifts in order to fulfill God's purpose for them. Christian leaders recognize the big picture and the scaffolding needed to achieve goals. Others are willing to follow those with this gift, trusting their guidance as they work to identify and pursue God's purpose in their lives (John 21:15–17).

### Using the Gift of Leadership

- ☐ Help with scheduling.
- ☐ Coordinate tasks.
- ☐ Be the organizer in your activities.
- ☐ Get others motivated and involved, help them live out their purpose.
- ☐ Volunteer.
- ☐ Take responsibility for a specific area of an activity.
- ☐ Help lead in a ministry of your church.
- ☐ Mentor others; help develop their leadership skills.

## Mercy

People with the gift of mercy desire to help others who have physical, emotional, or spiritual needs. They are compassionate and empathetic. They share words, acts of kindness, and care, working to eliminate difficulties for others (Matthew 25:34–36).

## Using the Gift of Mercy

- ☐ Volunteer at a food pantry or soup kitchen.
- ☐ Assist neighbors (take them to appointments, shop for them, listen to them, bring cheer, etc.).
- ☐ Work for agencies that help those in poverty.
- ☐ Help with home health care.
- ☐ Volunteer to minister to those in assisted living and nursing homes.
- ☐ Take care of others; be there.
- ☐ Always let those you love know you love them.
- ☐ Take meals to those who need them.
- ☐ Make and send cards to those in need.
- ☐ Participate in agencies that help with housing, meals, health, legal issues, or holiday needs for those in poverty.
- ☐ Recognize needs and assist when possible and where needed.
- ☐ Be sensitive; be a listener.

# Shepherding

Shepherds provide spiritual guidance for believers, with compassion and kindness. This is often in a long-term commitment (1 Timothy 4:12–16).

## Using the Gift of Shepherding

- ☐ Agree to lead a Bible study group.
- ☐ Teach a Sunday school class.
- ☐ Be willing to work with groups on a long-term basis.

# Service (Helping)

Those who serve are happy to work behind the scenes to further Jesus's mission of reaching others. They support the work of those who have gifts of working more directly with others (Luke 23:50–54, Philippians 2:19–23).

## Using the Gift of Service

- ☐ Cook a meal for those in need; deliver meals.
- ☐ Encourage others to work to meet their goals.
- ☐ Invite others to a church activity.
- ☐ Help with errands and daily needs of others.
- ☐ Share special treats.
- ☐ Clean up.

☐ Volunteer at church.
☐ Tutor.

## Teaching

Gifted teachers clearly communicate biblical principles and faith-based information using differentiated instruction to meet the needs of their learners while staying focused on biblical truths. Those with the gift of teaching have a strong understanding of teaching and learning strategies and work to promote the growth of their learners (2 Timothy 2:2).

### Using the Gift of Teaching

☐ Teach a Bible study class or a Sunday school class.
☐ Lead a small group.

## Wisdom

Those gifted in wisdom can discover the truth, even when it is buried in opinions. They examine ideas and information and help individuals and the church make wise decisions in a faith-based manner (James 3:13–18).

### Using the Gift of Wisdom

☐ Join a church committee and help with decision making.
☐ Be willing to listen to and share with others.

## Action Item

Take a spiritual gifts inventory online or in your small group. Identify your strongest spiritual gifts; list how you have used them in the past and how you might use them in the future. Choose one way and take action.

## My Prayer

Lord,

I have learned that You send the Holy Spirit to work in and through me. You have given me spiritual gifts that are unique, chosen especially for me. These gifts are what I need in order to serve You by serving others. Lord, help me to unwrap these gifts, examine and learn about them, and pray about using them. Help me to understand all of Your gifts, even if I do not have that specific gift, so that I have a greater understanding of how I will work with others as one body in Your name. May I take action in my life, incorporating my personal gifts into my daily life. Guide me as I try to courageously step out of the boat and make a difference in the world, with the gifts You have so lovingly put into my heart, mind, soul, and hands. In Jesus's name,

Amen

Chapter 8

# Dreams and Goals; Dream Big with God

Brothers and sisters, I do not consider myself yet to have taken hold of it. But one thing I do: Forgetting what is behind and straining toward what is ahead, I press on toward the goal to win the prize for which God has called me heavenward in Christ Jesus.
—Philippians 3:13–14

*Kathy Herrick*

# Drifting

The night is calm. No waves are lapping at the sides of the rowboat you sit in. You are content to just sit and let the world weave around you. It seems idyllic splendor to you: the moonlight playing across the soft ripples, the call of an animal far into the woods, stars twinkling above.

And then suddenly, the winds come, whistling through the trees that rim the lake, howling down through the valley splitting two mountains in the distance. Wild eyed, eager to get back to shore, you grab for your oars and only then realize they are not there. You look up, hoping to see a sail you can adjust to harness the wind, use it to move forward, but alas, this is a small rowboat, with no oars. And so you sit, let the winds come, let them blow you about, take you where they will, with no will or power of your own. You are at their mercy. Much later, the winds become softer, more gentle, and you think that at last, you have a hope to reach your goal, shore, home, but you find even then, you have no power to change the course of this boat, and so you drift and drift and drift.

Drifting; unfortunately, this is what happens to you, to your dreams, goals, and lives when you make no decisions, identify no dreams, set no goals, take no action. You are left to the mercy of life around you; you drift through life. Perhaps you have said, "Someday, I am going to _____." But if you never act on this, never embrace a dream, take action, your life will become one big "some day" forever. There comes a time when some day has arrived, when it is now or never. If you don't want to just drift through life, you need to be open to those dreams God has for you, open to hearing them, seeing them, embracing them, living them.

Build that life you want; go after your dreams. You have choices of your own, with God's help. You don't have to be what others are. Decide what means the most to you. Combat the human tendency to drift by identifying your dreams, setting your goals, finding the steps to reach them, and taking action. This chapter will help us all explore what our dreams may be, how they fit together with God's plan for us, the importance of dreaming in all areas of our lives, and how to set goals, establish those steps, and realize the dream.

# Paul: The Dreamer

Paul, God's man, was ever pushing forward, ever dreaming, ever believing that God had big things for him to do. Paul, who never knew the meaning of retirement, saw that he had to stretch to new ministries in order to touch more and more lives for Christ. He never forgot those he brought to Christ in his earlier ministries, providing for their support through letters and through others he brought into the ministry, but he was ever planning new mission trips, new ways to reach others for Christ.

Paul dreamed big for God. He was open, wide open to God, to how He might want to use him. He said, "Here I am," and he meant it. His whole life revolved around dreaming big for God and trusting God to support him as he worked to achieve those goals. For us, in our second half of life, God is still calling us to be like Jesus, be like Paul. Just because we are aging, taking on some aches and pains, it doesn't mean that the dreaming is done, that God has no purpose for us. He has a purpose for each of us, maybe a big purpose. Be a dreamer, like Paul.

## Your Dreams

If you're still alive, God has a purpose for you. I know you hear some people say, "But I can't because_____," but we have to think about how our dreams can modify, depending on our stage of life, our demands at home, our health. A big dream may be being a prayer warrior for God, spending a half-hour a day lifting up various others in prayer to God. Maybe it is to send notes, emails, and messages that you love someone, that you are praying for them, being the encourager. Or maybe it is a time to realize many are not able to serve in the same way, actively helping others, and your situation and health allows you to. Maybe it's your time to step out in that big dream and run a program, be an integral part of it. Regardless of where we are in the life journey and cycle, if we are still here, there's a reason for that, a purpose for us.

In thinking about this stage of life, I see more and more that one of our dreams should be to model for those following us. Even as we journey through this second phase, there are those who follow, taking their clues from us. Are we active, are we living our purpose, do we face the end of life with courage and hope?

Consider how God might use you, as you consider your dreams. Keep thinking, stretching, learning, being open to possibilities and potential. You never know what He has in mind. I have seen that over and over again in our Moving On Always Master Inspired program; women who weren't sure they could be a facilitator, for example, being just the warm loving touch the women in their group needed. I have seen it in myself. It took God and me two years to get our dreams together for me to coordinate the program with another woman. It happens in Bible study groups when people agree to facilitate and more. These are times when we should consider Peter stepping out of the boat in faith, to go to Jesus. Peter walked on water, but he had to get out of the boat. His dream was to be a water walker, and Jesus made that happen when Peter trusted Him and took that step.

## Reflection

What do you feel God may be calling you to do, to not just dream about, but to trust Him and take that first step?

_____

_____

## Holy Ambition

Holy ambition is aiming to be used in ways, by God, beyond what any of us can imagine. We all seem to have this little box in our minds. It is into that box that we put our expectations of God and our image of what He is capable of. We define what we think He is thinking, planning, considering, based on what we are thinking, planning, considering. It is truly chaining God down (and, in a way, chaining ourselves) to smallness, to what has been and is, and giving no opportunity for God to show us His might, His amazing power and love, and the wings He can give to any idea or any one of His children. We need to pop open the top on that box, flatten down the sides, let Him out. We need to fit on those wings, open up our hearts and minds, and get ready because it is in that attitude, with that ambition grounded in Him—Holy ambition— that our dreams will blow up into huge possibilities, and we will find the strength to reach out, touch them, embrace them, run with them.

Tom and I are retired, and lots of our friends are retired. We often hear, "I worked my whole life; now I'm going to play." I have often thought about God, wondering if there are points where He just figures He's worked enough, and He'll just turn His back and take a break from all of us. We all know the answer to that, and His model should be our example.

I do believe that God asks us to strive for balance in our lives, balancing service with me time, personal growth and revitalization time, leisure time, time with friends and family. I also think the lines between these pursuits can blur; time with family can be service time or revitalization time too, and so on. You are always ministering in your life. Your attitudes and behaviors, your priorities and actions, continually give off a fragrance, a flavor, show the fruit of the Spirit, the attributes of being a Christian—or not. But balance also says that we need to deliberately consider service, identify where and when we are serving our Lord by serving others, and if we are not in balance, change that.

I think of dreams sometimes; like hot air balloons, they're colorful, they fly, they are amazing (now don't be saying they are just full of hot air). I also think that there are times when the balloon rips, tough times when our dreams are deflated or we have to accept that maybe it's not the right time. There are also times when someone chooses to rip our balloon, let out the air, bring us down, surround us with negative words, but in those moments, I would counsel persistence. Sometimes, it feels easier to give up, that it's too hard to stick with it. But if you feel you are called to do something, if you have talked to God about it and believe it is in His will for you to be chasing this dream, if you expect great things, then persist and sail toward realizing that dream.

"But as for you, be strong and do not give up, for your work will be rewarded" (2 Chronicles 15:7).

God will provide what we need to realize our dreams in our ministries, if we trust Him. I had a dream of writing a book. My first thought was a children's book, but after I retired, I wasn't motivated to do that. Then came writing the daily on-line Bible studies, but I kept thinking there was more He wanted me to do, either with what I had already written or in a new format. We surveyed our classes at the end of each year, and they consistently respond that the text we were using did not meet many of their needs. We decided we needed to make a change but couldn't seem to find a book that fit. I felt a little nudge, and then some of the other women encouraged me to give writing new resource materials a try, and here I am, working on chapter 8. I needed the right people to encourage and push me, needed the "need" for a book, and then needed the words from God, and they are coming; in fact, they seem to be flying out of my fingers.

## Reflection

What dreams did you have in the past? Have you achieved your dreams?

_____

_____

## Beginning to Identify Your Dreams

"In their hearts humans plan their course, but the Lord establishes their steps" (Proverbs 16:9).

"Many are the plans in a person's heart, but it is the Lord's purpose that prevails" (Proverbs 19:21).

There are specific steps that we can take to gain information and self-knowledge that will help us identify our dreams. Use the following process and take notes to help you in the discovery process. Before each step, pray and ask God to guide you.

**Step 1:** Review personal information about yourself.

- Spiritual gifts. Take the inventory. Be aware of your specific gifts and how they can be applied in service. Weave your spiritual gifts into your dream.
- Fruit of the Spirit. Review each of these; do a self-evaluation. Which are your strengths, and which need more work? As you look at specific missions and dreams, consider where your strong areas are and how they would benefit a mission. Consider too how God can use a mission to strengthen your weaker areas.
- Who Am I? Review chapter 3; consider your self-identity and how being God's child can motivate the formation of your dreams.
- Passions and talents. We not only come with spiritual gifts, we also have a range of passions and talents. What are yours? What are your interests? What do others notice about your strengths and abilities? How will these answers help you be more successful in making your dreams come true?
- Activities in the past. Look back. What activities were you involved in? What did you enjoy? What would you want to do again? What do you know how to do that could be a part of reaching your dream? What skills have you developed?
- Desire. What is your desire? How do you want to minister? Who do you want to help? How do you believe you can help?
- What matters? Review chapter 1 and your list of what matters to you. How will a dream you are considering match the items on that list?
- Personality. What do you know about your own personality? Are you a people person? Do you like being with people? Do you enjoy working by yourself? How will your personality type help you achieve your dream?

**Step 2:** Talk to persons involved in various ministries and those trusted people in your life. Ask them what they see as your strengths, how they see you serving, where they see a match of your unique gifts and the needs in the ministry or mission areas.

**Step 3:** Read and study the Bible, spiritually based books, information about various ministries and mission projects.

**Step 4:** Make a list of the needs that have been opened to your eyes: your family, neighborhood, church, local area, country, the world.

**Step 5:** Make the connections; where do the needs match your ability to help meet them? Pray some more. Identify your dream. Ask for God's blessing on your dream, and ask Him to be with you as you work toward your dream.

**Step 6:** Write the goals you will need to accomplish to make this dream come true.

**Step 7:** Make a plan. Lay out a doable plan to reach each goal; write it out, step by step. Share this with a friend for accountability.

**Step 8:** Take the first step toward your dream.

**Step 9:** Persevere, keep going, keep God close. Know that you and God are going to accomplish something amazing. Don't give up.

**Step 10:** Celebrate each successful step toward realizing your dream.

"May He give you the desire of your heart, and make all your plans succeed" (Psalm 20:4).

## Dream Big for God

Our lives are often a series of small dreams, and we can make a difference, one small step at a time. But consider: God may have a big dream for you. Paul had important work to do where he was, but he never stopped dreaming and stretching to reach more people. How can we stretch our dreams, touch more lives, do even more?

About ten years ago, a woman in Chicago made a few scarves and donated them to a homeless shelter and low-income schools. It spurred her on to let others know of the need and invite them to join the ministry, and it grew. She was willing to go from small to great because she followed the dream and listened to God.

You may be working in a ministry right now, but we need to remain open and available. God may have something ready for you that is bigger, that touches more lives. He may be preparing others to take your current place and will lead you to new efforts that you are the right one to help with, to lead, to start. God may be calling you to do something you never thought of before.

Be open to it, willing to let go of what is known, comfortable, the same, and see new possibilities ahead. The need to let go isn't just about past events. Sometimes, we have to let go and let God lead others into the ministry we've been a part of, because He has something new, different, big, and important ready for us.

We are each unique, with something (a gift, personality trait, passion, interest, or a combination of these) that makes us prepared to do a particular mission God has in mind. I like to think about God having a dream He needs someone to share with Him. There are people all lined up. "Will you share?" He asks. "Will you? Will you?" Down the rows He goes until He finds someone to say, "Yes, Lord, here I am, make the dream mine too." Be open to the dreams He offers you, be willing to see how they fit into your skill set, your spiritual gifts and where you are in life. Be willing to say yes.

"Trust in the Lord with all your heart and lean not on your own understanding. In all your ways submit to Him and He will make your paths straight" (Proverbs 3:5–6).

## Guidelines for Attaining Your Dreams

- ☐ Make the dream about God, not yourself.
- ☐ Reach beyond what you initially thought was good. Go for the best.
- ☐ Identify your dream, the goals, the action plan.
- ☐ Keep your goals measurable. How will you know when you have accomplished them?
- ☐ Keep God in control of your dream.
- ☐ Use your gifts, talents, desires, passions, skills, and experiences to do the most for God and His children.

## Helping Others Reach Their Dreams

God asks us to be encouragers in the area of dreams. Look around. Who has a dream you could help them realize? Who is yearning toward a mission but needs some encouragement to keep making those steps? Who is working in a mission and needs more hands to realize the dream? Who may need some financial support or need someone to listen, to help them truly identify the dream and consider what goals and steps to take in order to embrace that dream? Be open and aware of others around you: their dreams, their purposeful living, their hopes. Be a part of that; invest in that; use your time, talents, and treasures to not only further the dreams, goals, mission that God has for you, but to further those for His other children too. As you bless, you will be blessed. As you move self out of the center of your life, you will find fulfillment as never before. Be a dream catcher, for someone else too.

## Reflection

Who in your life has a dream that you could help them realize? In what way can you help them?

_____

_____

## Goals

God: Focus on God's love for you and how amazing He is, how big God is. Let Him out of your box; let His dreams for you out of your box. He is much bigger than that; there is nothing He cannot do. He is always faithful with you. He wants the best for you.

Open: Be open to God. Your dreams and goals are not about self; they are about God and His will for you. Be humble and open to His leading.

Attitudes: Take on the attitude of courage, determination, and belief. Make "I can do it" your answer to those who question. Work diligently, with focused and sustained efforts. Believe. All things are possible through our Lord who loves us.

Love: Be surrounded by God's love as you identify your dream(s), establish goals, and develop action steps. As you take those steps, let His love shine from you onto others.

## Goals in All Areas of Our Lives

New Year's Eve resolutions don't seem to last much more than a day. That resolution to become healthier through eating more nutritious food and exercising kind of flies out the door when the New Year's Day football-watching banquet is spread out. They are notoriously not healthy, but the point here is that there are important goals that we should be setting, not just in our direct ministry and spiritual life, but also in our personal relationships with others, in our healthy living, and in other areas of our lives. God loves us as whole people. He loves all aspects of us and wants those dreams for us to be realized in all areas.

Following are some examples of how others have used dreams and goals to find a purpose and make a difference in their life, personally and for others. Perhaps it will help give you some ideas of what your dream may be and how to set up goals and steps.

**Dream**

**Making Prayer Quilts for Those in Need**

Goal: Learn to quilt

Steps:

- Buy a sewing machine.
- Take a sewing class.
- Take a quilting class.

Goal: Be a part of the Prayers and Squares Outreach Ministry

Steps:

- Find out the schedule, talk to the leader, and attend a meeting.
- Help cut fabric while learning to sew and quilt.
- Look for a mentor to help me make my first quilt.
- Listen for those who are in need and refer them to Prayers and Squares.
- Make praying for those referred an integral part of my prayer life.
- Keep quilting and donating and praying.

**Dream**

**Have a More Harmonious Home Life**

Goal: To be patient with my husband

Steps:

- When the toilet seat is up, take ten deep breaths and be quiet.
- Use "I" phrases when talking about tasks and not "you" messages.
- Decide what matters and let what doesn't matter go.
- Encourage and compliment Tom; listen to his golf stories.

Goal: To keep the house clean and in order.

Steps:

- When I use something, put it away.
- Keep my project clutter in my project room.
- Buy more storage containers and use them.
- Take a deep breath and remind myself that it doesn't have to be perfect.

**Dream**

**Have a Close Relationship with My Grandchildren**

Goal: To stay in touch with each of them

Steps:

- FaceTime with them once a week.
- Write each a note or card and send snail mail every few weeks.
- Make photo books each year of the time together.
- Spend one-on-one time with each one, take walks, play games, and listen.

- Celebrate their accomplishments.
- Write my story to share with them.
- Display their artwork and photographs.
- Hug them, tell them they are loved, and spend snuggle time.
- Share that Jesus loves them.
- Take them to church, and let them see me worship.

## Action Item: Now or in the Coming Weeks

Identify a dream for a mission and one for a personal dream. Identify goals with steps to reach each. Take action on one of the steps.

## My Prayer

Lord,

Please keep me from drifting and point me toward the purpose you have for me. I want to be useful to You because I know You love me. I want to do work that will glorify Your name. I have to get out of my boat and try new skills and ideas. I have to let You out of the little box that I put You into and realize how amazing and capable You are, what magnificent things You can do. Help me dream big for You. As I plan my course of action, please guide my steps. Help me make a significant difference for others, perhaps just one small step at a time, but many small steps means a big difference. Please open my mind and heart to let You in to do Your best work in me.

In Jesus's name,

Amen

# Chapter 9

# Finding Your Purpose; Serving Our Lord

The King will reply, "Truly I tell you, whatever you did for one of the least of these brothers and sisters of mine, you did for me."
—Matthew 25:40

## The Great Commission

### Luke 24:13–45, Matthew 28:18–20

The tomb was empty, the linen clothes neatly folded, but the disciples still asked, "Where is the body?" They seemed to be wandering about, asking that question over and over, until Jesus appeared to them, with a few more lessons to teach, more commandments to give, needing to convince those doubting disciples that He really rose from the grave and would soon ascend into heaven.

You are there, on the road to Emmaus, a dusty road, with rock outcroppings on either side and a spring ahead. Walking with your friend, you shake your head in dismay, sharing the story on the tip of everyone's tongue: Jesus was crucified, He died, His body had disappeared; what a mystery. Were the local detectives on it? Probably not; they were aligned with the Romans and the Sanhedrin. What a mess. A third man joins you, asks about your conversation; you relate the news yet again and say how your hope that Jesus was the redeemer of Israel has been dashed now. You share the women's story, which no one seems to believe. You stop at the well for water and then walk on home and invite this man in. He blesses the bread and breaks it, and then you know: It is Jesus.

You are in a room with the disciples; the door is secured against those who would harm you. Suddenly, a man appears. You are scared; it must be a ghost, a spirit. Will you be harmed? You draw back in fright. The spirit speaks. He speaks of not being troubled, asking why there are doubts, and then He shows the piercings in His hands and feet, and you know: It is Jesus.

His teachings in those last earthly days were not just for the disciples; they alone could not carry the cross into the future, be His hands, feet, voice, and heart. It would take all of His followers over the years, including us. Yes, the words of Jesus are for us:

"Peace be with you."
"As the Father sent Me, so send I you."
"Receive the Holy Spirit."
"Forgive."
"Feed My lambs and tend My sheep."
"I will gird you."
"Follow Me."

A handful of words, perhaps not His exact words, but the powerful message throughout is clear: We are to be faithful believers, follow Jesus's example as we live our lives, be filled with the Holy Spirit, be filled with the strength only He gives, take care of and forgive others as He did, and know that we are commissioned to serve God in the world, just as Jesus did. Powerful; we are being sent out, just as Jesus sent out the disciples: "Take up My Cross and Follow Me."

This chapter will discuss finding our purpose in serving God and exploring ways to bring together our spiritual gifts, dreams, and goals in order to live out the personalized commission He has for each of us.

## Preparing to Serve

In the last eight chapters, you have been challenged to focus on your own unique life story. You have been asked to analyze what matters to you, what past experiences you've had, what is your identity, how the fruit of the Spirit fit into your life, how to bloom and find contentment despite your circumstances, how to develop and maintain Christian friendships, what your unique spiritual gifts are, and how these all work together to become your dreams (and the goals and steps you need to take to attain these dreams). All of these have intertwined together to lead you to this examination of a broader picture, looking at what service for the Lord is and to encourage you to begin discerning what God is calling you to do for Him, now and in the future.

Reading scripture is one way to discern what service God may be calling you to. The Bible is a living, timeless document. Messages were not just appropriate for the time in which they were written; they are still full of information and direction for each of us today, for the world today. Jesus also left a part of Himself to live in us: the Holy Spirit. The Holy Spirit is there as you read the Bible. There are verses that stand out in highlight for each of us as individuals, because the Holy Spirit knows these are the verses with messages we personally need to focus on. Through these specific verses, we are being guided and given instruction on how He wants us to serve Him. We are being prepared for the mission ahead, getting ready to act, getting ready to serve.

Paul's response to God's call to serve is a good example for us. Look at his life: He was chosen by God and challenged, through the loss and regaining of his physical sight, to see that the true vision needed comes through the lens of Jesus. Paul was filled with the Holy Spirit, and his sins were forgiven. He felt deeply the commission from God to serve. He was hopeful, believing that through living out his purpose, traveling, preaching, ministering, serving others, he was living out his commission, he was serving a living God, he was making a difference. Through this sacrificial faithful service, his own faith grew and was strengthened.

In examining Paul's life, we see the parallels to our own lives. We too are chosen by God, asked to view life through God's lens. We too are given the Holy Spirit, and our sins are forgiven. We too are commissioned to serve God, to hold close the hope for the future and our ability to impact that future for others in a positive way, in His name. We too serve a living God and can make a difference. Serving God in a sacrificial way will also make our faith grow and strengthen.

Most of us are in the second half of our lives. We want to make a difference now, but finding our commission is something we should pray about and be willing to wait for discernment to unfold. God may have an answer right now: sign up to help with MOAMI next year, go home and take care of an ill spouse today. But maybe, like Paul, He is asking for patience, study, prayer, and a willingness to step away, find quiet moments to listen, and then to act. God will show you the way if you are quiet and listen. The world is a noisy place; we tend to talk before we ever hear, so this quiet listening needs to be a very deliberate activity.

Teri, a special friend, shared that every year on her birthday, she goes for a walk and has a special talk with God. Different than her daily prayers, this is a time to review the year before, look ahead to the coming year, revisit those dreams and goals, and consider what they need to be as her tomorrows unfold. What a precious tradition: spending time with her true Father, on the day He first shared her with the world, just the two of them, in the most important of ways.

Service is a very personal and unique experience. We are each so different, which is how God planned the body of Christ to be. These differences make life interesting, allowing us to fulfill the wide variety of needs of others and together complete the picture of God's family and mission. How we choose to serve will be different from how others serve. Our backgrounds are different, gifts are different, circumstances are different. It is important that we not compare our service to others, feeling we are not doing enough or that others are not doing enough or too much. None of us knows the true picture of what others are living with and how God is calling them. We can share opportunities, but the decision to serve belongs to each of us individually. What He does ask of us is to help each other prepare to serve and to be in prayer for each other.

## Reflection

What have you identified as your purpose?

_____

_____

What ideas do you have to help prepare you for your service?

_____

_____

## What Is Service?

There are lists of activities at every church, and when we read them, we can begin to feel something like guilt because we're are not signed up on more rosters. But think about Jesus's ministry; He was not on any roster, except God's.

Examining Jesus's life, we see He modeled giving and serving by doing it constantly. It was a part of who He was and in His every interaction with others. Joining together and creating committees and organizations, collecting food, or working together to do something is not wrong; not at all. There is power in collectively doing something. But Jesus was always teaching, especially the disciples. He gathered them together, taught them about service that comes from being His, not from doing it because you are supposed to do it, or because you think it is expected of you, or from guilt or peer pressure. You perform the service because you love God and just want to share that with others.

He had a small group, the disciples. He nurtured them, taught them, and then told them to turn and go out into the world, often in different directions, to serve His people. We are to do the same. We are to learn about God, learn about service, then turn and live it in our everyday lives.

Our definition of service needs to broaden. When we listen to someone whose loved one has died, giving them an outlet for sorrow, that is service. When someone listens to our troubles and helps us see a path ahead, they are serving. When we talk with a friend who is ill or afraid of death, that is service. When we care for an older parent or little grandchildren, that is service. When we are kind to someone in the store or help someone whose car has broken down, that is service. When we share a meal, that is service. We don't tend to recognize those times, but we minister and share messages of God's love with our daily demeanor and actions, share His love as we support others.

We often put the idea of service in a box, like we sometimes do with God. We give it a narrow definition. We need to let possible ways to serve God out of our small box and become more aware of just how big and amazing our God is. We need to see how we can serve in a multitude of ways, all day, every day, even without our names always on a roster.

Empower each other to serve the Lord, every day, in every way.

## Here I Am

Purpose.
Do all the good you can,
by all the means you can,
in all the ways you can,
in all the places you can,
at all the times you can,
to all the people you can,
as long as you can.[1]
(Attributed to John Wesley)

### Isaiah 6:1–12

The Panama Canal was an amazing feat: finished more than a hundred years ago, at a time of limited technology, limited knowledge about illness such as yellow fever and malaria, and unbelievable hardships, and yet they pushed on to create that amazing wonder. Workers on the Brooklyn Bridge would go down to the floor of the river in a wooden crate, to dig; can't even picture that one. But look at the bridge today, which will still be standing for many more generations. In the face of insurmountable odds, they carried on and triumphed in both of these cases. There are times when we think there are insurmountable odds in our lives, but we need to pray and trust God and His power and strength.

"Here I am, Lord." God uses us. Here I am, Lord, for the canals and the bridges of my life and the ones in the lives I touch. Even when it seems like there are mountains, disgruntled people, and rivers that rush madly at us, He is there. Philippians 4:13 states, "I can do all things through Him who gives me strength." Just four words: "Here I am, Lord." Not "when I'm ready," "someday," "if I feel better," "if I can get my finances in shape," "if I can find time," "if there's

---

[1] "Purpose" is generally attributed to John Wesley, although there are people who believe it is a compilation of his writings and sermons.

the right technology," "if there's no disease threat," "if it's safe," "if someone asks me," "if they are nice to me," or whatever. Just "Here I am, Lord."

Sometimes, we go through painful experiences to get it, to pay attention to God, to see what He has for us to do. God does not cause bad things to happen, but He does teach us through them. There are lessons each time life is hard, and there are blessings in those times too. He asks us to see and hear, not just in the real sense, but with our hearts and minds. We must have faith and trust Him. He asks that we open up our hearts and minds, to see through His lens, and to truly hear what He is asking of us.

Mother Theresa said, "Do things for people not because of who they are or what they do, but because of who you are."[2] I would add, "because of *whose* you are."

## Service Isn't Always Easy

### Luke 19:1–10

We saw the Zacchaeus tree in Jericho; I could hear voices: "What's Jesus talking to that sinner for? Can you believe it, he's actually walking alongside of that man. Do you know what I just heard? He's going to have dinner at his house. You mean he is actually going to step into that house, break bread with that sinner? Doesn't he know that our kind doesn't do that, that we are better than those people?"

If we never hang out with sinners, if we only surround ourselves with Christians and God's people, who will do God's work among the unsaved? Who will shine God's light on them and share His love with them? Who will say, for that part of His mission, "Here I am, Lord?" Who will stand as an advocate for children in situations where the home is so dysfunctional the children have been removed? Who will make and serve food for the hungry? Who will help construct homes for the homeless and support them as they and their children try to learn how to do life? Who will share clothes, buy new tennis shoes, be a listening ear? Who will make sure there is running water and electricity, health care, sanitary conditions? Who will see that all children have good educational opportunities and see the future as a positive? Who will share hope for a better tomorrow on earth and in heaven? Who will share the good news of God's love?

Jesus's example: right here with Zacchaeus, it's our job. Here I am, Lord, send me. Send me to the food pantries, the soup kitchens, Habitat or Helping Hands homes, the clothing donation boxes, the schools as a volunteer, to be a guardian ad litem, the prisons, the homeless shelters, the abused women and children shelters. Send me, Lord. Send me.

In the words of Lily Tomlin, "I always wondered, why somebody doesn't do something about that, and then I realized I am somebody."[3] We are all somebody.

### John 4:1–30

Jacob's Well: How exciting it was to read this scripture. I was there, at Jacob's Well. I sat beside the well (now in the basement of a church). I dipped out some water and brought it home in a

---

[2] Mother Theresa. There is some confusion and disagreement about quotes from the words and writings of Mother Theresa.

[3] Lily Tomlin.

little earthen jar. The woman was from Samaria, of mixed heritage, not Jesus's kind, and she was a woman. He asks for a drink; she is shocked that He would even speak to her. But the water Jesus spoke of was not what I dipped up, not what is in my earthen jar. It is the living water of Jesus, the water of everlasting life, the water that washes away all of our thirsts, forever. This is what He was offering the woman and offers us. She listened, even though she was perplexed that He was even talking to her; she listened with an open heart and mind.

Are there times we don't speak to others because they are different, because we aren't supposed to? Are there times we don't listen to others for the same reason? Are there times when the message of God needs to go through us to those who aren't like us or times when He has a message for us from someone unexpected?

Did the Samaritan woman just listen up and head on home for the evening? No, she heard and became a part of the mission. She hurried home and told others, shared the good news, brought others into Jesus's fold. What an example she was for us. Listen to the messages at worship, or think about the messages God is sharing with you as you read scripture, and then don't just leave it at the door, in the book, on the computer, as you go on with your life. Take it with you, spread it around, share the good news that is Jesus, bring others to the well.

When we share with others, we may never know how far the ripples of that pebble in the pond may go. Look at where Jesus ministering to the Samaritan woman went. We may never know who we touch, who will be changed, who will carry the message even further. We have to be open, honest, and minster to all people with faith and trust, knowing God's mission is being furthered.

## Luke 10:38–42

Awhile back, I attended a "Mary Retreat," basically a retreat with no agenda, no plan, no have-tos. We were encouraged to just come and share, to experience, to decide in the moment what we'd do. But as we were struggling to shuck off our natural tendency to be Marthas, I started to think that Martha gets a bum rap. If we were all Marys, sitting, listening, then the practical would not happen: the hands in the dishwater or on the tools, the work done so that others with different gifts could apply their gifts. Mary and Martha were certainly women with very different spiritual gifts.

As we consider our previous study of spiritual gifts, we know that different gifts are given to different people. Mary was gifted with praise and worship. Martha's gift was service and helping. Both loved Jesus.

The Marthas of the world make sure the doors are open, the coffee made, the lights on, the bills paid, and more. They're the backbone of the practical daily functions of the church. They organize mission trips and keep an organizational structure within the church. They know where the keys are, make sure the church is locked up when everyone leaves, and see that the lights are turned off. The important thing for Marthas is to make sure that in overseeing the organization, the structure, the management, they don't lose sight of what the true mission of the church is; all of these tasks are important if they further the mission of ministering to God's people and bringing others into the fold.

And Marys: Their minds and hearts are totally focused on worship, on love, on the mission of sharing God's love and light. They often miss the practicality of the needs of the church and individuals and can upset the applecart of organization when they don't follow rules and guidelines. That said, they often ask the important question: "Why not?" Marthas need to consider and answer that question; sometimes, rules need to be broken and guidelines bent, when it's going to make a difference in the lives of others, when the good news message of Jesus will be furthered. Marys also need to recognize that the work of the Marthas often make possible their work of sharing the good news of Jesus.

The bottom line is that whether you are a Mary or a Martha, or some of both, regardless of what your gifts are, what service God has called you to do, that you do whatever it is, in the spirit of praising and worshipping our Lord, with sincere and giving hearts. We need both Marys and Marthas, working together, loving and praising God.

## Reflection

Are you a Mary or Martha? Why did you choose the one you did? Can you be both? How can you praise God in either role?

_____

_____

## Give It Away

My house, my car, my bank account, my time, my stuff, and more: I have been successful. I have been able to do something. I won this. I accomplished that. Each of us is raised and lives with the idea that this is all our stuff, that it's our own talents that get us ahead, and we are pretty quick to say, "I'm too busy." Our own time, talents, treasures. But where do all of them come from? Where did all this time, all the talents, and all the stuff come from?

God gave us everything; it was first and foremost His. He is loaning all of it to us. He has gifted us. He never expected us to hoard our time, talents, and treasures or to exhibit selfish and self-promoting tendencies. His expectation is that we will use His gifts in His service. What He asks is for us to be willing to exhibit a selflessness in using what He has given us, in service to Him. Do we worry what is in it for us, or do we see a need and step up to be a part of the solution, without a thought of self? We have the privilege and responsibility to use the resources God has given us, to share His good news.

Several years ago, I felt a call to lead a women's ministry program. I struggled, because the day of the class was my neighborhood golfing day. It took me six months of "talking" to God, arguing, pleading, negotiating, to finally say, "Here I am" (and mean it). When I called and volunteered, I was told someone else had been chosen. Picture that: All that struggle, all that heartache, and I wasn't needed.

I had to have a few more talks with God before I got it. He wasn't asking me to hold that position right then. He had been asking me to be willing, willing to give up the grip I had on my time on that day of the week, my insistence that I had to play golf that day. It was a big lesson for me, being willing. This can be true, too, about our finances. Does He want us to give all of our money away, or is He asking that we be willing to share our finances with others, knowing He will show us when and where to share? I began to look at service and donations differently; serving from a right heart, being willing, was often as important as being a part of the actual mission itself. There are lessons He has for us, always.

(An aside: A year later, I did become a part of the women's ministry program as co-chair, in God's time and way. Another lesson to learn.)

## Kinds of Service

"I serve a risen Savior, He's in the world today." "We've a story to tell to the nations." These lines are from songs most of us are familiar with. So where and how do we put it all together, serving our living Savior and telling the story of His love?

### On a Personal Level

Our mission sometimes is close to home—or right at home. Raising children or caring for an aging parent or ill spouse are all missions that God gives us. They often become all-consuming, keeping us from other types of mission work, but God understands and expects us to take care of needs at home first. There are also ways to support other missions, even when we have to be at home. We can always pray for others, for missions of the church, close by or far afield. We can support other missions with our encouragement, letting others know that we believe in them and their work for Jesus. Another way to support service from home is financial. A donation may be just what is needed to further the work of an important mission.

### Ways to Serve

- ☐ taking care of grandchildren, parents, spouse
- ☐ donating finances to a mission
- ☐ encouraging others in a mission or needing help, sending emails, connecting through FaceTime, phone calls, notes, cards
- ☐ knitting or sewing at home and donating items to those in need
- ☐ making and sending cards to those in need
- ☐ praying, praying, praying
- ☐ helping a neighbor in need

### In Your Church Community

In every church, there are various ways to serve. Some are at the church itself, such as volunteer positions in the office and on the grounds. There is ushering, serving coffee, teaching Sunday school, handing out registration forms, serving at the visitors' desk, and more. There are also ways to serve in the worship service, such as music, lay leader, and reading the scripture. Check with your church office for options specific to your church.

## Ways to Serve

- ☐ volunteering in the administrative offices
- ☐ helping in a variety of ways at the weekly worship services
- ☐ helping with programs for the vulnerable in society
- ☐ serving as a teacher
- ☐ helping take care of the physical building
- ☐ being a part of programs at the church, ushering, food preparation, serving
- ☐ praying

## In Your Wider Community

Some of the outreach programs in your community may be supported by your local church. Examples are meeting educational needs through a tutoring program, medical needs through a local clinic, feeding those in poverty through a soup kitchen. Check with your church and your community offices for a list of programs that accept volunteers and support. Googling for information or checking in your local newspaper may give you other options. I read a newspaper article in Michigan about a Birthday Box program for at-risk children, which led me to help start that program in our area in Florida. I also read about the "My House Ministry" program, which provides housing and support as women and children transition out of abusive situations; this led to our Florida knitters making winter scarves for these individuals. Be open, make connections, read, explore with an open mind and heart, see the seeds God may be planting. Let everything be a possibility to consider.

## Ways to Serve

- ☐ volunteering at the local school
- ☐ donating food to the local food pantry
- ☐ being an intake person at a local free clinic
- ☐ helping at a local homeless shelter
- ☐ helping build or rehab homes and mentor families
- ☐ praying
- ☐ being a part of the local prison ministry

## Nationally and Internationally

We often hear people say we need to meet the needs of those in our local area and that we need to quit sending support to other countries. God tells us differently. He says to take care of those around us and also to send support to others far away. Paul was supported in ministry close to home, but followers also gave him support to give to those he ministered to on his mission trips far away. We should always look around close to home, see the needs, and do something about them. But likewise, we need to look beyond what is close, to countries far away, and see how we can help meet needs there too. We have the resources, the time, the talents, and the treasures to do both. If you consider some of the poorest areas on earth have no affluent neighbors nearby to help them, it's us or it's nobody.

Oftentimes, we cannot go to other places, but there are still ways to support service there. We can pray; we can participate in programs with our donations, such as a well project in the Congo; we can give support, financial aid, and encouragement to missionaries, just like the early believers did for Paul.

## Ways to Serve

- ☐ praying
- ☐ donating financially
- ☐ going on mission trips
- ☐ sending needed supplies

## How Will You Serve?

### Discernment

- ☐ Pray, watch, listen, read the Bible, talk to Christian friends; consider your spiritual gifts, your experiences, talents, what matters, your dreams.
- ☐ Take a quiet walk in nature and talk to God.
- ☐ Look at where you are right now, what God has planted in front of you.
- ☐ Say, "Here I am, Lord," mean it, and be prepared to be amazed at how blessed you are when you serve others.
- ☐ Listen and watch for open doors; follow those dreams.

## Action Item

List service ideas you have for yourself personally, in your church, in your community, and in the greater world. Choose one and take action by working to address a need.

## My Prayer

Lord,

I want to be able to say, "Here I am, Lord, use me." I want to be a faithful believer and follow Jesus's example as I live my life. I want to be filled with the Holy Spirit. I need to bring together my spiritual gifts, dreams, and goals in order to live out the personalized commission You have for me. Please give me patience to study, pray, step away, find quiet moments to listen, and then act. Thank You for all the blessings that You give unselfishly to me, every day of my life. Lord, I need You. Thank You for always being there for me to lean on. Praise God!

In Jesus's name,

Amen

Chapter 10

# Your Legacy: Pass It On

But you, Lord, sit enthroned forever, your renown endures through all generations. Let this be written for a future generation, that a people not yet created may praise the Lord.
—Psalm 102:12, 18

*Kathy Herrick*

## What's This Thing Called Legacy?

Imagine the following obituary that might be found in any newspaper:

**Brown:** Mary Brown, born May 15, 1940, to Robert and Betty Allen, died June 22, 2017, in Cincinnati. She is survived by her husband John and two children, Susan (Bill) Jones and Joe Brown. Her service will be Tuesday, June 27, and burial will be in Greenville Cemetery.

Mary Brown: Who was she? She was born, she lived, and she died, and yet, as we read her obituary, there are very few clues about her life, who she really was, what mattered to her, how she lived out her values and her mission, what aspects of her character, beliefs, values, passions, interests, and most importantly faith are being left behind, in her children and in others her life came in contact with. The clues are sketchy; she had parents, a husband, two children, but what was her legacy? Who was she, what mattered?

Legacy, the most powerful product of life, is handed down from generation to generation, passed individual to individual. We have been left the legacy of those who have gone before us and those whose lives have touched us. We are in the process of leaving a legacy in those who are in our lives now and individuals who will come after us. We reach out and grasp the memories, wisdom, character, faith, and beliefs of those in our past, and we stretch forward and share with those who are coming behind us. It is the heritage that we hand to the future; it is a way that our own personal life stories live on. In some way, by leaving a legacy in others, it allows us to feel a kind of immortality, that our lives and how we lived mattered, even though we are each one small person in the big sea of humanity. Those we touch are different because of how we lived, because we touched them. We need to feel this, believe this. Our lives matter.

Some believe that legacy has to do with wills, trusts, and legal papers pulled out after someone dies. This couldn't be further from the truth. It is all about life and living, learning from the past, living life in the right now, and preparing for our own future and that of others. We are in the process of embracing the legacy from others every day, and we continually pass our own legacy to others our entire life, to family and to those whose lives we touch in all kinds of ways; it is the fragrance that we leave behind, with everyone.

As I look back, I think about my parents, grandparents, and the ancestors in our family who lived so many years ago, those who lived and died long before I was born. I only know of these individuals through faces on aged and tattered photos or maybe just a name on the family tree. I know a few stories about some of them, told to me by my grandparents, but I believe I intimately know these people that I've never met because I knew my grandparents and my parents, knew what mattered to them and their beliefs and values. I know it was the legacy of my far-back ancestors that nurtured those beliefs. That legacy was passed to my grandparents and parents; they passed it to me, I pass it on to others and in some way, my ancestors do live on.

Legacy: Whether we are aware of it or not, we are leaving one; it may be positive or negative. Look to history to see examples. Contrast Mother Theresa's legacy and Hitler's. We need to consider what kind of world we want to live in and leave behind, and what part we play in that with our choices. Legacy is an integral part of being human, and without the sense that we have something to pass on, we can become self-centered and lose some of the meaning of life. Legacy is about our relationships, families, friends and our very spirit.

What we leave behind, our legacy, is a personal decision for each of us. We need to be deliberate in searching out the meaning of our own life and articulating what matters to us. It is not something to be found in our obituary (although there may be clues there). Our legacy is not something that happens when we die or as our will is read or as someone sorts through our possessions, although all of those will give clues. Do we want them to have to search for what our legacy is, or do we want to be deliberate about articulating it and demonstrating our legacy through how we live, how we touch others? Our legacy is making the personal decision, with the help of our Lord, about what kind of person we want to be and be remembered as. Are we leaving a fragrance that tells others of our accurate legacy?

"For we are to God the pleasing aroma of Christ among those who are being saved and those who are perishing" (2 Corinthians 2:15).

While most of us aren't famous (we won't find our names in a "*Who's Who*" book), our loved ones know us well. They may only hold us in their memories for a generation or two, and then we will fade, but there is and will be meaning to our lives because our legacy, our gift to the world, to others, won't be lost. All of these people will carry on, will live life differently because of us.

In this chapter, we will reflect together on what a legacy is, what we want our own personal legacy to be, and how to be deliberate about leaving that message with others whose lives we touch.

## Whose Legacy Has Touched My Life?

Recently, Tom and I traveled from our winter home in Florida to our summer home in Michigan, and we made a brief stop in Nashville, Tennessee at the cemetery where my parents are buried. My eyes lingered on Dad's information: born on May 1, the same day that I stood gazing down at his headstone, the one hundredth anniversary of his birth. The day a baby comes is a joyful day, a happy day; he was the first child, first grandchild, a healthy child. I can just imagine. My eyes slid to that other date, twelve years back, and I remembered those last moments and the heartache of that day.

But my dad, the real essence of who he was, the legacy he left, I realized, was in that dash in between those two dates. I ran my fingers back and forth over that dash, remembering the twinkle in his blue eyes, his wit, compassion, integrity, love, remembering all the actions of caring for us, helping others, hearing his voice telling me about life, the way he lived out his faith, and more. Our legacy is in the dash, in how we live each and every moment between that first date and the last; we are living the dash right now. What we do and say matters, tells our story, leaves our legacy, our fragrance behind.

## Reflection

Take a few moments to look back at an influential person in your life. What do you believe was their legacy? What specific actions did they take, words did they say, that left you with the knowledge of that legacy? How did their legacy help shape you and make you a better person?

_____

_____

_____

_____

## What Is Jesus's Legacy for Me?

"God forgave you. Follow God's example, therefore, as dearly loved children and walk in the way of love, just as Christ loved us and gave Himself up for us as a fragrant offering and sacrifice to God" (Ephesians 5:1).

"For God so loved the world that He gave His one and only Son, that whoever believes in Him shall not perish but have eternal life" (John 3:16).

As we have read, legacy is the sharing of beliefs, passions, faith, values, character, and what matters most in one's life. It is a leaving of one's fragrance with others, both now and in the future. It is an affirmation that one lived, and lives on, in this world and beyond.

Christ is our greatest example of a life well lived, with God at the center and love permeating every aspect of His earthly existence. He left a powerful legacy. We need only to look to God to see the roadmap, the model, the message of legacy that can help us choose our footsteps and our direction, help us live in a way that shares the legacy of love with others. Christ left us a legacy of love and service and asks that we turn and leave a legacy of love and service in others too. Will others know about love because we have lived, just as we know more about love because Jesus came to earth and lived? Will others know more about sacrifice and selfless giving because we lived, just as Jesus modeled that for us? Will others know about the good news because we have shared it, just as Jesus shared that with others and through them, with us?

"To this you were called, because Christ suffered for you, leaving you an example, that you should follow in His steps. He committed no sin, and no deceit was found in His mouth. When they hurled their insults at Him, He did not retaliate, when He suffered, He made no threats. Instead He entrusted Himself to Him who judges justly." (1 Peter 2:21–23).

In each place we trod in our lives, we leave footsteps that the waters will not erase. They may blur the edges, but the essence will still be there. Our part of building on the foundation laid by our Lord, and continued by those who have come before us and living around us, will remain as a support for others. The fragrance that we pass on—God's fragrance—will linger in the essence of others.

A prayer attributed to Mother Teresa, but also considered by some to be one written by a Catholic clergyman, tells of being so full of the fragrance of God that self will disappear and others will instead see only the light and love of God. It goes on to conclude that our praise of God is visual, seen in how we treat others, how we impact their lives, in what legacy we leave in them. It's a huge responsibility: to so live as to continually shine God's light, share His love, being open and willing, letting Him take center stage in our lives, letting everything we are and do radiate from Him.

## Reflection

What attributes (fruit of the Spirit and more) of Jesus do you want to include in your legacy? What are some ways you can share Jesus's love with others?

## How Will My Legacy Impact the Lives of Others?

All the years living our dash not only shares our essence, it impacts others' lives. They go on to live differently, to touch others' lives differently. In their dash, our legacy goes on through them to others, even though our name and face may not be known. We are different because of the dashes of others. Others are different because of our dash. Now is the time to be deliberate, to consider what we want that legacy to be, and to be sure that is the message we are radiating.

Sometimes, we have done our very best, have worked hard to be a conduit of love for others, have tried to follow Jesus's example, have given the message of love, kindness, peace, and hope, and yet the very ones we hope most to be speaking to do not seem to be listening. I've been there; I've been in the situation where a loved one turned their back on who I was, what I lived, my faith, love, legacy. I get how hurtful that is. I know the feelings of frustration and helplessness, of not knowing where to turn next. It was a hard lesson, but I know God told me to let go, put this relative in His hands, to be true to His legacy and mine, and leave the ministering to this relative to God's way and time. It was one of the hardest things I have ever done. I let go. I know the years of pain, and I know the answers are not always easy. Somewhere in their lives are the seeds we have planted, God has planted. God may be preparing someone else to nurture those seeds of legacy, and that means trusting God, but also believing that your legacy is in there someplace, tucked in their heart by God.

Our legacy can also change the life of someone we are not directly related to. We may touch that person in a way that changes the direction of their life; in so doing, we may change the legacy they are living and leaving. Our legacy may move down through generations that we have no blood relation to. This kind of legacy passing can be as important as leaving our legacy with the generations in our family. In all ways, with all people, remembering the words of John Wesley.

The main character in a book I read recently spoke of writing her legacy in a sentence or two and tucking it into her child's pocket, symbolic of living life so that one's legacy is in reality tucked into their hearts. I love that image: the idea that we have lived our legacy so truly and honestly that it's implanted deep in the hearts of those we love and touch.

## Reflection

What would you write, in a sentence or two, about your legacy to tuck into the pocket of someone you love?

_____

_____

_____

## What Is Your Legacy?

"One generation commends your works to another; they tell of your mighty acts" (Psalm 145:4).

Recently, I dug through a box of mementos, and as I shuffled through the papers, I began to see our legacies: not what we did, but our sons' reaction to it. I found it in their notes, cards, and letters. I happened upon a Father's Day card Rich made for his dad, where he listed his characteristics from a history whiz, to honest, intelligent, loving, faithful, funny, giving. His note, "You are all of these, but the most significant is you are always THERE." Legacy.

There was another note from our son Joe on my birthday: "I am inspired by your work, your faith, reverence and drive in trying to make this world a better place, your devotion to family." Legacy.

Figuring out your own legacy is taking stock of your life: the pluses, the minuses, the accomplishments and defeats, what you have learned, the impact you have made on others, what is ahead, what your hopes and dreams are. It is reflecting on your deeds, the people in your life, your work, ideas, and choices. It is stepping back and considering what has defined your life, what has shaped you into the person you are, what matters most to you, how your faith weaves through all.

## Reflection

Take some time to remember. If you have old cards, notes, letters, and email, look through them and consider the mark you have made on others. What is it they say about you and to you? What messages were you trying to give, and what messages did they hear and see? Do they match?

Consider the following questions:

How do you want the world to remember you?
Does the way you live your life reflect that?
Do you live with integrity, courage, love, and faith?
What do you highly value?
What matters the most to you in your life?
Who do you want to pass your legacy on to?
What excites you in your life and brings you joy?
Why did you pursue your career?
When is a time you stumbled, fell, failed, were disappointed?

If you were to live life over, what would you change? What would you keep the same?

What are you grateful for?

What has helped you in the tough times? What helped you in the joyful times?

## How Will I Pass It On?

"Love the Lord your God with all your heart, with all your soul and with all your strength. These commandments that I give you today are to be on your hearts. Impress them on your children. Talk about them when you sit at home and when you walk along the road, when you lie down and when you get up" (Deuteronomy 6:5–7).

Being aware of the legacy you hope to leave will help you recognize and take advantage of opportunities to more fully live it and pass it on to others. You will see teachable moments to pass on what is most important to you.

Recently, I mentioned the word "legacy" to my son Ben, the father of three little ones. I was still thinking about that idea of writing one's legacy in a sentence or two to put in a child's pocket, so I asked him what he'd say my legacy was. He didn't answer that; instead, he spoke about his own legacy. He said that our conversation made him realize that what he does every day is laying out his legacy for his own children and for others. He felt he needed to define what he wanted his legacy to be and then look at where he spends his time, how he lives his life, his priorities, how he treats others, to make sure the messages are left in ways that transcend time.

At first, I was a little impatient. I had wanted to talk about my legacy, and here he was talking about his. But then I realized that his legacy is about my legacy, for who he is, what he believes in, how he shares that—the seeds he plants in others, the fragrance left when he passes by—are all reflections of what I have planted in him, the fragrance I have left with him. You should have this conversation with your children and those close to you; a good place to start is how they perceive your legacy and what legacy they hope they are leaving in others.

Generations spiral back from us and spring forward. Who we are reflects our forebearers: what they chose, how they lived their legacy. Who our descendants and those whose lives we touch will become, will be shaped by how we live our lives, the faith and beliefs we carry and live out, the love we extend.

Last Sunday, our pastor's message focused on legacy. She said, "The good news is always one generation from extinction," pointing out that if we aren't deliberate about passing the good news on to future generations, it will die on the vine, for how will they hear and know it? What if the generation of our great-grandparents had not passed it on? Where would we be in our faith walk? Things to think about. We have the responsibility to teach forward, to turn and look ahead, to be sure there is no extinction of God's good news.

"We will not hide them from their descendants; we will tell the next generation the praiseworthy deeds of the Lord, His power, and the wonders He has done" (Psalm 78:4).

## Passing on the Good News

One day, my dash will end, but we live on in those we love and who love us. Consider the way our parents live on, through us. When a kind word is on our lips, it is our mothers or fathers speaking too; when our hands take up the work of helping others, our parents' hands lay gently on ours; when a tough situation is ahead of us, our parents' voices are in our minds, reminding us that we are capable, that we can do it, and that God is nearby, strengthening us. We are reminded, too, that now the responsibility for sharing the good news is ours; it is time to be deliberate and thoughtful, not only about what that legacy is but how to share that legacy, loud and clear.

In this season of life, we are blessed with more time to reflect and more of life to reflect on, for wisdom comes with age and experience. We can reflect on who we have been, where we are now, what we want our lives to be, and how to live more purposefully in the future. It's a time to evaluate if our lives mattered and to get busy and make sure the rest of our lives do make a difference. If we are not satisfied with our legacies, it is a time to shift. If we consider that our legacies are our most powerful statements about the definition of the lives we have lived, it is critical that we give this topic attention and make sure our life practices match our wishes for legacy.

What are some ideas for sharing our legacies? There are everyday messages, how we live our lives, and what others see as we make choices and deal with what life hands us. There are opportunities we can create. An example is the little girl my granddaughters and I help fund a Christian education for. Our little girls send letters and pictures to this little girl, and she sends letters and pictures back to them. A goal for our girls and our little sponsored girl is to know about the importance of caring for others, about love, and about the importance of education and learning about Jesus. They know this is important to me too; it is a part of my legacy to them.

What are other legacy-sharing ideas? Celebrate birthdays and special days together. Show up when someone in the family is doing something special. Play games together; share family stories, jokes, and funny times. Do something silly, do something athletic, make music, go to the beach, take a boat ride, or make cards and letters. All give a message of a legacy of valuing family and love. Pray together. Worship together.

## Ideas for Passing on Your Legacy

- ☐ Invite those you love to articulate their own legacies.
- ☐ Spend time together and talk with each other.
- ☐ Use technology like FaceTime, email, and texting.
- ☐ Make correspondence boxes with paper, pencils, stamped addressed envelopes, and art supplies for writing to each other.
- ☐ Share family stories.
- ☐ Read books together.
- ☐ Record the family's oral history.
- ☐ Digitize and share old photos.
- ☐ Share family recipes and talk about who they come from.

- ☐ Preserve family memories; make photo yearbooks.
- ☐ Keep a journal.
- ☐ Save old letters and type them up into a booklet for your children.
- ☐ Learn and write down the story of family keepsakes. Photograph them and make a booklet of the photos and stories.
- ☐ Fill in a blank memory book.
- ☐ Make a family tree.
- ☐ Take trips together to family spots, hometowns, cemeteries, and schools; share stories.
- ☐ Do crafts and projects together.
- ☐ Volunteer together.
- ☐ Pray together.
- ☐ Share a Bible study together.
- ☐ Sponsor a family reunion or other celebration.
- ☐ Write letters and send cards with personal notes.
- ☐ Let your family see you giving to others and supporting them.
- ☐ Talk about your volunteer activities.
- ☐ Share your faith.
- ☐ Share family traditions: the real tradition or stories of the traditions.
- ☐ Make handmade items for your children, grandchildren, and significant others.
- ☐ Make a photo scrapbook together of a family adventure.

## Action Item

Define the legacy you desire to leave. Create an action plan with specific ways you will pass your legacy to others. Take action.

"For what I received I passed on to you as of first importance: that Christ died for our sins according to the Scriptures" (1 Corinthians 15:3).

Pass it on. Commit today that you will live for what matters the most in your life, with your choices and priorities aligning with the legacy you are choosing to leave. May you put the Lord at the center of your life, basing your legacy and your future on His love. Legacy: You are a part of something much larger than self; your footprints in the sand will not be washed away. Your mark for Jesus, your mark on those whose lives you touch, will live on. Embrace your future.

## My Prayer

Lord,

I want my life to be worthwhile. I will be handing my heritage to the future generations, so I want my legacy to be a solid foundation for them to build their lives on so they are prepared to continue passing it on. Remind me often that my legacy is about life, living, learning from the past, living for the present, and preparing my generation and future generations to carry on faith-based beliefs and values. Help me focus on what my legacy is, always living in a way that shares a clear message about what matters to me. Let me live my legacy now so that my faith in Jesus shows by my acts of love and kindness. Please help me send my own personal message that radiates love, kindness, and a belief in You and that shares what matters most to me. In Jesus's name

Amen

# Chapter 11

## What I Learned

Thoughts of others on their self discovery journey through this study:

I have learned …

- that listening is the most important part of my conversation with God, then discerning, then acting on that understanding.
- that my faith has been strengthened. I have felt the presence of the Holy Spirit guiding my journey.
- that friends are important. The Holy Spirit works through others and speaks to us through others.
- that listening is a true art form.
- that sharing leads to caring and deep bonds with friends and God. I've never felt so connected and uplifted, totally blessed.
- the meaning of "love."
- that God is always with me, and having a friend nearby makes life so much easier.
- to try and be patient and to trust God. God answers prayers, and we have to trust He will in His time.
- that through trusting God, He changes you in ways you would never believe, creating opportunities for us to grow.
- there's nothing better than being with people who love and follow Jesus.
- the joy of the Lord.
- that I've been given wings. I prayed for direction, and God placed me where He wanted me.
- to take all my troubles to God in prayer, and that there is always support from Christian friends. We are always growing.
- life is easier when you open up and trust God.
- I need to let go and let God take over various aspects of my life.
- the joy of being with Christian sisters and the importance of sharing ah-ha moments as well as grief and disappointment.
- to pray more often, effectively, and openly.
- how strong faith can be and how helpful a deep faith is in my life.

- to keep trying to learn, over and over, that it's not about me; it's about what I can do with the help of God.
- the value of Christian friendships and starting anew.
- to be more open and aware of my feelings about God.
- to listen, share, and extend the hand of friendship to new women.
- to be flexible.
- that anything is possible; there are no limits.
- that the best is yet to come.
- that growing and serving the Lord is an amazing and uplifting experience.
- we can all grow where we are planted and can move on, let go of the past, and look to a positive future.
- to make my faith stronger, to reflect daily, and to share.
- to be grateful for my blessings and to have no regrets. God is good.
- to be open to all possibilities since everything is possible with God. He will give me enough strength to do it.
- the importance of trusting the Lord to move me forward in His plan for my remaining days.
- the important thing is God in the center of everything, and prayer is the answer to all.
- to have time for others. Each person may be the most important one, the one Jesus wants me to listen to.
- that I may not be where I need to be, but I am so much better than where I used to be.
- how best to serve God at this time of my life.
- the importance of looking to my legacy.
- it is important to take time to be quiet and listen to God's whispers.
- that when I let God out of the box, He freed me too.
- that we're not alone; God is always with us, showing us the way.

And now it's your turn. What have you learned about life's journey, about being God's child, and about being in the family of God through this study:

I have learned _____

_____

_____

_____

_____

_____

With deep and sincere thanks to:

Lynda Ruter, who wrote the beautiful prayers at the end of each chapter.

Teri Quick, Phyllis Sommerman and Pastor Marilyn Anell for editing and reading for content.

Gemma Benjamin for help with support materials and her wit that always kept me centered.

The leadership of the Moving On: Always Master Inspired classes for their encouragement to chase the dream.

Christian friends and the daily Bible study readers for their belief and encouragement.

My husband, Tom, and our family for their patience, encouragement, and love.

The staff at New Covenant United Methodist Church in Florida for their support and encouragement, particularly Barb Prindle and Ellen Pollock.

The first class—both participants and the leadership—to use *Embracing Our Future* at New Covenant United Methodist Church, for their feedback and recommendations.

Our Lord Jesus Christ for His ever present guidance and push to be partners in the dream of making this book a reality.

Printed in the United States
By Bookmasters